POWER
IN
WOODWORK

POWER
IN
WOODWORK

GORDON STOKES

Model and Allied Publications Limited
13–35 Bridge Street, Hemel Hempstead, Hertfordshire, England

Model and Allied Publications Limited,
Book Division, Station Road,
Kings Langley, Hertfordshire,
England

First published 1974

ISBN 0 85242 344 6

Printed by Henry Garnett & Co. Ltd., Rotherham & London

Contents

Introduction

The intense fascination of natural wood as a material for constructional purposes, carving, turning, model making, or whatever takes the fancy cannot be denied, be it the humble pine or the most exotic of tropical timbers, and once a man falls under its spell he rarely breaks away. True, there are some excellent man-made materials used by the woodworker and extremely useful they are, but nothing is quite like natural wood— there is something special in the feel of it, its smell, its colour, and the life it retains. A man could devote his entire life to the study of timber and how to work with it, but he would not have enough time to learn it all. The shaping, cutting, smoothing, polishing, and finishing of a project are things no man should miss, for there is a special joy and peace to be found in making something from wood, whether it is done with hand tools, power tools, or a combination of the two.

It matters not that the finished job is not perfect for he must come to realise that perfection can never be attained; what does matter is that he should learn to use and to enjoy using tools and making things from wood—any sort of things as long as they are shaped as he intended. At times there can be a deep and wonderful satisfaction in the craft, and yet at others all is frustration for nothing will go right.

In days long gone, men had time to study their craft and to put much of themselves into their work, for then they were judged by the quality of it rather than the quantity as is rapidly becoming the case . . . the pace of life has stepped up to an alarming degree and "near enough" is the order of the day in far too many cases. I have some Jacobean chairs which have seen a great many years roll by and will see many more for they were made with pride and craftsmanship and not thrown together. They will still be good chairs long after I have gone on my way.

The changing times have, however, brought about another alteration, this time to the good. This is that the average man can no longer afford to send for a carpenter when there is work to be done around his home— prices are prohibitive, and so he has been forced to learn at least something of woodworking and in many cases he has discovered great pleasure and relaxation in it.

I have little time for the moaners who say that the advent of power tools has taken the skill out of woodworking, and that only the man working with hand tools can be a craftsman. This is sheer rubbish. In the proper use of power tools, with accuracy, safety and a good finish to the job, there is a great deal of skill. It is needed in the setting up and maintenance of the tools, in the sharpening, grinding, and honing of their cutters, and in the correct application of the tools to the job. Power tools are great time and energy savers, and I maintain that a bad worker will turn out a bad job even with the best power tools available. There is still plenty of room for ingenuity and inventiveness, and a man can work to high standards with power tools just as in hand work.

The aim of this book is not to teach woodwork but to show what tools are available, their capabilities and limitations, how they should be cared for, and how the maximum amount of benefit can be derived from them with the minimum of effort, bearing in mind the all-important subject of safety.

It is my earnest hope that this book will help the beginner in the difficult matter of deciding what machinery he should buy, what he can afford to buy, and more important still, what he cannot afford not to buy. If it succeeds in this and helps him to get the best results with less risk of injury, then it will have been well worth the long hours that have gone into its composition.

Gordon Stokes, Conderton, 1973

CHAPTER 1

Drill and saw attachment

Fig. 1 Bosch Combi drill, with casing cut away to show armature and gears

THE modern electric drill is a wonderful thing indeed. It gleams invitingly at us from the shop window, simply bursting with enthusiasm to get into our homes with all its attachments and effect a marvellous transformation. Given a good drill and the correct attachments for it, plus the necessary skill to set them up and use them, this is quite possible. Unfortunately it is also possible and in fact quite easy to buy the wrong type of drill for your purposes, and a number of attachments which will not be of very much use. Where it is intended to purchase the more expensive industrial tools many makers will send a representative, on request, to demonstrate the tool at your home. This is well worth arranging if it can be done, since these demonstrators know their products well and can give a good many valuable hints and tips. If your requirement is for a small drill which will do the odd jobs, and you have no intention of buying much in the way of accessories or going in for sawing or drilling in metal, one of the cheaper drills will fill the bill well enough.

It is vital to give the matter very serious thought before committing yourself, however, because there is every chance that before long you will find the need for a stronger tool. In changing over you are likely to lose money because the secondhand value of an electric drill is never very high regardless of its age. If it is old its low value will be obvious, whereas if it is fairly new the prospective buyer is apt to think that it has had a hard time and you are therefore dis-

Fig. 2 Saw attachment for Wolf drill, showing washers which secure blade, and tilt mechanism

posing of it. You may well have purchased some accessories for it, too, and it is possible that these will not be suitable for use with the new one.

It is doubtful whether the average home user really needs a four-speed drill, or indeed whether he ever uses such a tool to the limits of its capabilities if he does buy it. Two speeds will usually suffice, and certainly so if the main use of the tool is to be woodworking. A pistol grip handle is best for normal use; the back handled drills are normally in the industrial range and intended for use where heavy pressures have to be applied. From the point of view of safety in insulation, an all-insulated drill is best because even the chuck is isolated from the current supply, and you would be safe even if you were to cut through a power cable—although I am not recommending the practice.

Fig. 2 shows the *Wolf Sapphire* saw attachment (see also *Ch. 5, Fig. 9*). As I said earlier, the saw is likely to be the first accessory bought for the drill so we may as well

look at it in detail. In *Figs. 3 and 4* I have shown the checks which should be carried out before the tool is actually put into use. If any of these checks should reveal faulty adjustment it is vital that this be corrected at once or accurate work will be impossible. Once properly set up these little attachments are accurate enough for precision work, but if they are incorrectly set they will be a nuisance.

Some self-powered portable saws are illustrated, but in general the remarks which now follow apply to either type. The power of this type of saw is relatively small by comparison with a static sawbench. The optimum peripheral speed of the saw expressed in feet per minute is 9,500 and small saws like this do not attain this figure. It is therefore considered best to allow the blade to have maximum projection through the sole plate even when the material being cut is quite thin, since this means that less teeth are in contact with the wood and so there is less strain on the motor.

By virtue of the direction of

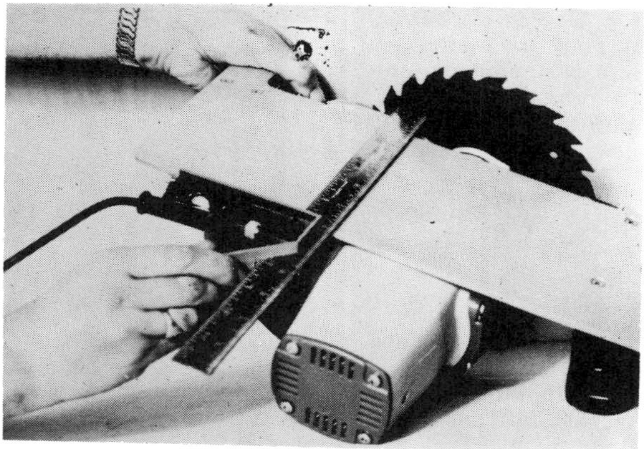

Fig. 3 Checking for
exact blade alignment
with sole plate. This is
vital for successful
work

Fig. 4   Checking for
ninety degree angle
between blade and
sole plate on a self
powered saw

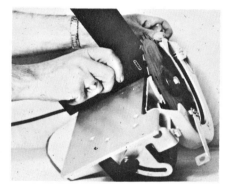

of all there is freehand cutting to a marked line *Fig. 5*. The line is drawn on the wood and the sole plate of the saw is guided along it, keeping a mark or notch on the front edge of the sole plate aligned with it. Ripping can be done to a marked line if necessary although there is usually a ripping guide provided, *Fig. 6*. If the timber being ripped has a straight edge good results can be obtained, the guide being kept in contact with the edge all the way through the cut. These guides are secured by means of a thumbscrew and can be adjusted as required. It is, of course, important to see that the screw is securely tightened before starting the cut.

rotation of the blade, two things happen. One is that the sole plate of the saw tends to be held down to the work, and the other is that the teeth are coming upwards through the wood, and so all marking out is done on the reverse side. If the material is marked out on the face there will be a rough edge, and this of course applies particularly in the case of cutting man-made materials faced with plastic laminates.

Ripping and crosscutting can be done quite well with saws of this type, and there are three basic methods. First

Another method, also very useful on occasions, is to construct a "T" guide. It is shown in *Figs. 7* and *8*. This is made with the cross piece a little longer than necessary and the saw is then run along, first on one side and then on the other, with the edge of the sole plate in contact with the stem of the guide. It is most important that the edges of the stem piece are straight and parallel. The

Fig. 5   Power saw ripping to a marked line. Notch or mark on front of sole plate is aligned with the guide line

Fig. 6   Wolf Sapphire portable saw in use with ripping guide (shown bottom right)

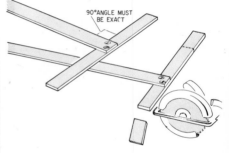

Figs. 7 and 8   Construction of "T" guide for use with portable saw. When guide is first used blade will sever cross piece as shown. Sole plate is kept against stem.

cut is taken right through at the ends so that the cross piece is severed by the blade. If this guide is now clamped across work to be cut, with one end of its cross piece aligned with the point at which it is desired that the cut should finish, the saw can be run across, contacting the stem of the guide with the sole plate all the way, and the resulting cut will be perfectly accurate.

In the cutting of a very large sheet of material it is sometimes more convenient to clamp a long batten right across the sheet. In this case the end of the cross piece can be used

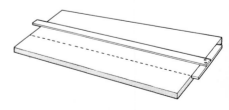

Fig. 9   End of guide is aligned with mark on work. Very accurate cutting can be done this way

Fig. 10   Use of "T" guide to establish
position of batten when crosscutting
a wide board

to locate the point at which the batten must be clamped as in *Fig. 10*. This type of guide is not accurate unless it is accurately made, and it must be checked with a square before use, to make quite sure that the stem is at right angles to the cross piece.

Another factor which must be considered when using this type of saw is that the wood being cut has to be held very securely, so that there is no chance at all of its moving during the cutting operation. Also, it must be supported high enough above the bench to prevent the blade from fouling anything underneath. Another important point is that adequate support must be given when cutting large workpieces so that the work does not droop as the cut proceeds, thus pinching the sawblade. This applies particularly in the case of sheets of hardboard or thin ply which sag easily, and can cause the saw to buck in a dangerous manner.

The majority of modern portable saws have thermal cutouts to protect the motor in such cases, but there is no need for things like this to happen

at all, if a little thought is given to the job beforehand. The sawblade must not be allowed to become blunt, and the rate of feed should be such that the note of the motor does not drop appreciably. One soon learns to listen to the sound of this and to feed the work accordingly. Even though the majority of drills today have welded commutators, which can take a lot of punishment, there is no need to abuse the tool.

Freehand cutting to a marked line is suitable for work which is not critical, but where accuracy is required it is best not to use this method, since it does not always give perfect results. A batten clamped across the job to guide the edge of the sole plate is a better bet, but allowance must be made for the distance from the edge of the sole plate to the blade, and for the thickness of the blade itself.

Portable saws are frequently used for cutting large sheet material down to working sizes, and this can best be done in one of the two ways shown in *Figs. 11* and *12.* In the first instance the sheet is resting on blocks so that it is clear of the ground, and there are blocks at either side of the point at which the cut will be made, so that there will be no tendency for the work to sag as the cut proceeds. The cut starts at the bottom of the sheet, either running the sole plate along a batten clamped to the wood, or cutting freehand to a guide line. This method works well.

An alternative is to have the batten crosswise to the sheet, running the saw along it, and putting a wedge or two in as you go to prevent the top

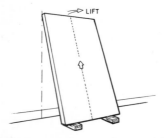

Fig. 11 ·Large sheets of material are stood on end with blocks under to permit start of cut. Blade projects just through the wood, which is lifted away from wall at end of cut

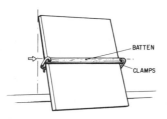

Fig. 12 Horizontal cut across a large board. Saw runs on batten, cut is wedged open with chips to prevent jamming of blade

Fig. 13 Setting tilt of sole plate on a Bosch saw by means of a hardboard template

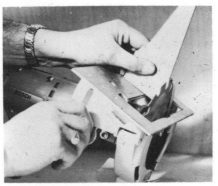

piece from dropping and nipping the blade. Of the two I must say that I prefer the former method, though both are in common use. If the sheet is small enough it can be supported on blocks and laid flat, but this is impractical with big boards.

With both drill-driven saw attachments and self-powered saws there is provision for tilting the sole plate to permit angle cutting. It is not always safe to rely on the markings, and I find it better to set the angle by means of a hardboard template, a number of which I have made and kept.

Sometimes one reads of saws of this sort being clamped upside down in a vice, and used in the manner of a sawbench. A horrible accident could result quite easily, and since most makers can supply a small sawbench with its own rip fence and mitre gauge for a pound or two, the idea is utterly stupid. The procedure for setting depth of cut and the tilt of the sole plate, varies very little among the different makes. It is of course important to clamp the holding screws firmly before using the tool. For the man who is not yet ready to go in for bigger equipment, the *Mini-Planer* is a useful little tool. It has an adequate guard which is spring-loaded, and which is automatically pushed back as the wood is fed to the cutters, returning after the wood has passed over. The cutter head is $2\frac{1}{2}$ in. wide, and in view of the fact that the power source is a drill, this is enough. I would recommend it to any newcomer to power work, because it will teach him a lot which will stand him in good stead when he goes on to a bigger machine.

Fig. 14   Bevel cross-cutting with Wolf power saw

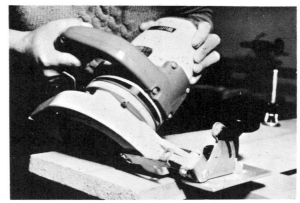

Fig. 15   Depth of cut on Sapphire saw is controlled by a clamping lever, and alteration to the setting is simple

Fig. 16   Mini Planer set up with Bosch drill. Both planer and drill support clamp must be bolted to bench. Keep blades very sharp, and cuts light

CHAPTER 2

Other drill attachments

IN this chapter I will stick to drill attachments, leaving the operation of a sawbench until later in the book. A sawbench is a very versatile thing indeed, and many users are not aware of its full potential.

Before going on to discuss the attachments for electric drills, it may be as well to think for a few moments about speed and how it is controlled. With a single-speed drill this is obvious enough—one plugs in and pulls the trigger. There will also be a locking pin for the trigger, *Fig. 2,* which enables the tool to be used in a bench stand leaving the operator with both hands free. Some drills, like the *Black & Decker DN70V* in *Fig. 3* and the *Stanley Bridges Colour-matic,* have facilities for varying the speed over the range. In the *Black & Decker* drill this is arranged through the trigger, the motor running faster as the trigger is pulled harder, and vice versa. The *Stanley Bridges* drill has a knurled disc in its body, being painted in sections of various colours. The speed of the motor will vary according to the colour selected, and this is an ideal drill for the man who wants to use a small lathe, *Fig. 4* and *Fig. 5.*

Other drills have two set speeds, like the *Stanley Bridges Lectronic, Fig. 6,* which gives low speed on first trigger pressure, and high on the second. Four-speed drills can be bought having the same sort of

Fig. 1 Wolf four speed drill mounted in its pillar stand. This is a reliable and useful all-round tool

Fig. 2   Trigger-locking pin, indicated
by pencil, will keep the motor running

Fig. 3   A Black and
Decker DN70V drill,
with variable speed

Fig. 4   Stanley-
Bridges Colourmatic
drill in close up,
showing disc in rear of
casing which controls
the speed

Fig. 5   Colourmatic
drill as power source
for a small lathe

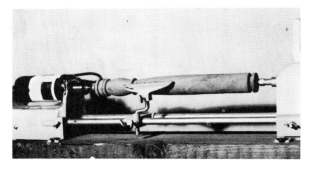

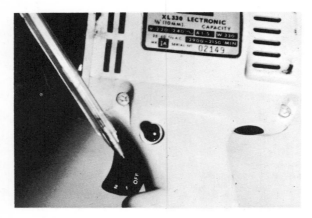

Fig. 6 Stanley-
Bridges Lectronic drill.
Pen indicates two
speed trigger control

Fig. 7 Stanley Swirlaway sanding
attachment allows sanding disc to
remain flat when drill is tilted

Fig. 8 Wolf Sandiflex foam drum
sander in use

Fig. 9 A self powered
orbital sander. Very
useful when all the
rough work has been
done

system, but in addition there is a gear change lever on the drill, altering the speed through a gearbox so that there are two speeds in the high ratio and two more in the low. For the moment, then, let us look at the other attachments for the drill, to see how else we can utilise this little maid of all work. With a circular saw and a *Mini-Planer* we are off to a very good start, but there is plenty more yet.

What about sanding facilities? Sanding by hand is a long job, and rather an uninteresting one. First we have the well known circular disc with a rubber backing pad, which beginners seem to like, though they quickly discover its limitations. For rough sanding it is a good tool, though it is next to useless for any form of finish sanding no matter how skilful the operator. It is difficult, if not impossible, to prevent it from gouging into the surface of the job and thereby doing far more harm than good.

There are variations on this, *Fig. 7*, one having a ball joint to allow the drill to swing slightly while the sanding pad remains flat, and with a cushion of foam rubber behind the abrasive paper. There is also the foam rubber drum type of sander which is good, inasmuch as it has a belt fitted round a foam rubber pad, and so the path of the abrasive grains can follow the grain of the wood. It has one disadvantage which one learns to live with and eventually to overcome, this being a tendency for the belt to run off the drum in one direction or the other. This is overcome by tilting the sander slightly.

Fig. 8 shows one of these, the *Wolf Sandiflex*, in use. It is not necessary or desirable to apply heavy pressure with this type of sander.

The rigid type of disc sander which has a metal plate with an abrasive disc attached to it and a table on which the work is placed for sanding, is quite another matter. I will leave it until we get on to the bigger machines, since there is a good deal to be said about it.

The tools so far mentioned are, in the main, for fairly rough abrasive work, but we do use sanders for the actual finishing of projects. The finishing sanders are the orbital type which has a flat base with the abrasive paper stretched over a foam rubber pad. Orbital sanding attachments are available for drills, *Fig. 10*, and there are some forms of belt sander intended to be driven by drills but these seem to me to be a trifle primitive, so I will leave discussions on belt sander details until later (for illustration, see *Ch. 8, Fig. 7*).

The drill driven orbital sander, however, is an important item of the drill owner's kit and if correctly used will save him hours of work and enable him to produce really excellent finishes ready for staining, paint-

Fig. 10 Orbital sanding attachment by Bosch

ing, polishing, or whatever. This type of sander is not designed for the rapid removal of wood, and it sometimes happens that a man buys an orbital sander only to be disappointed with it because he feels that it cuts too slowly.

The truth of the matter is, of course, that this tool is the last one used when all the rough sanding has been done, and the difference it can make to the work then is quite remarkable. Unlike the foam rubber drum sander or the belt sander, the path of the abrasive grains is in tiny circles, the pad being made to orbit by means of a small cam. Little or no pressure is needed with this tool as its own weight is enough, and it should be lifted from the work now and again to allow the dust to escape and to avoid clogging the paper.

Abrasive paper is still frequently referred to as sandpaper, although in fact this is wrong, for the abrasive papers used in machine sanding today are a far cry from the sandpaper and glasspaper we used years ago. They are made up with a very strong backing paper and abrasive grains of garnet or aluminium oxide. Garnet is red in colour, and aluminium oxide a dark brown. Garnet is very efficient and suitable for most applications about the home, while aluminium oxide costs more but lasts longer, and is favoured for use on industrial machines.

The matter is further complicated by the fact that one can purchase abrasive papers classified either as "open" or "closed coat", and the beginner is likely to be a little confused by this. One decides which is the more suitable according to the work to be done. Personally I keep supplies of both. Closed coat paper has more abrasive grains to the square inch, and so in theory it will cut faster. When used for hand sanding it is perhaps the better choice, but open coat paper is best for machine work. The fact is that having the maximum number of grains per square inch may sound a good idea, but there is a very real problem in that such papers tend to clog quickly, particularly when used on pine or other resinous woods, and as they become loaded with wood dust and resin, so their cutting efficiency deteriorates.

Another matter with which the beginner has to become familiar is the question of the actual size of the abrasive granules, regardless of whether the paper is open or closed coat. Here the best advice is to remember that high numbers represent fine papers and the low numbers coarse ones. I use really coarse paper such as 36 on very infrequent occasions, most of the stuff I use is 60 or 100, together with some flour grade, which as its name implies is very fine indeed.

No doubt the day will come when manufacturers will standardise their methods of describing the grain size of their products, but it is regrettable that at present there are several different systems in use. It is worth remembering that coarse paper will eventually wear its way down to medium and medium paper will wear its way down to fine, so if you are as parsimonious as I am you will not throw your paper away until it

Fig. 11   A variety of boring bits and cutters for use in power work

Fig. 12   Drill attachments. Left to right: impact attachment, twist drill grinder, right angle drilling converter

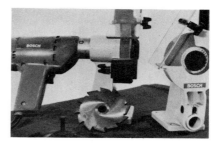

Fig. 13   Grinding attachments. Comb joint cutter and rubber disc sander in foreground

Fig. 14   The Screwmate set, by Stanley

begins to fall apart.

There is a wide variety of drill bits available for use with power tools, *Fig. 11,* and the type used depends to a large extent upon the job in hand. We will be coming back to this later in the book, so I will not enlarge upon it here. One or two other useful items which you may like to have around for use as and when needed are such things as paint stirring rods, *Surform* drums for cutting wood away quickly, wire brushes for removing rust and generally cleaning up metal, grindstones, polishing mops, and so on. Some of these are shown in *Figs. 12* and *13.*

Where a lot of screwdriving has to be done, the *Screwmate* set by

Stanley, Fig. 14, is a real blessing. I built a canoe recently, using what seemed to me at the time to be thousands of brass screws and these *Screwmates* were worth their weight in gold, since they will in one operation drill the correct sized holes for thread and shank, and countersink for the head. They will also cut a hole in the surface of the work so that the screw heads can be buried, and by using *Stanley* plug cutters, *Fig. 15,* cross-grained plugs can be cut to fit the holes and hide the screws.

There is another item which will be found really necessary when polishing or grinding has to be done, this

Fig. 15   Stanley plug cutters, used in cutting cross-grained plugs to hide screws

being a bench stand for the drill. This leaves the operator with both hands free to manipulate the work and so greatly increases the versatility of the drill.

Rebates can be cut in all sorts of ways, as we shall see, but for the man who is limited to an electric drill there is the choice of a saw attachment or the tiny rebating devices, *Fig. 16*. The other operation which he may need from time to time is grooving, and again the saw can be used, or there are special little tools to attach to the drill for this job.

Fig. 16   A typical rebating attachment for use with an electric drill. Two cuts are required to remove the waste

For both grooving and rebating, wobble washers can be attached to the sawblade so that it does in fact wobble as it revolves, the edge moving in an arc from side to side. The degree of wobble can be varied by moving the washers which set the blade at an angle to the spindle. Rebating in this way is not too easy, and it will be found necessary to clamp a straight piece of timber to the sole plate of the saw so that it can run along the edge of the wood being rebated. The use of wobble washers with drill-driven saws is not really a very good idea, although it does work. The point is that the blade is being made to remove quite a lot of wood at one pass, and normal sawing is hard enough work for a drill anyway, so unless the rate of feed is very steady there is a good chance of overheating the drill motor.

A better way of rebating with a portable or drill-driven saw is by making two cuts to remove a corner of the wood. This requires very accurate depth setting and it will usually be necessary to use some scrap wood when cutting into the edge with the work in the vice to give the sole plate of the saw sufficient support. The special rebating tools for the drill are much easier to use, and in fact they are very efficient. They are in reality tiny circular saws having facilities for setting depth and width of cut, and rebating with them is simplicity itself.

The cutting of grooves, something the woodworker frequently has to do, has similar solutions. If you do not want to overload your drill by using wobble washers, a batten can be clamped across the work and the groove made by a series of cuts. Either the batten can be moved over by the thickness of the blade each time or a packing strip equal in thickness to the sawblade can be inserted between saw and batten after each cut. The *Woden Corrucut, Fig. 17,* has a special corrugated blade which takes a wider cut than a normal sawblade, and its construction is similar to the rebating attachments in that its depth of cut can be set, and the blade can be moved over after each cut until the desired width has been reached. It can also be used for rebating, with its fence attached.

One or two other items designed for use in conjunction with electric drills are shown in the accompanying illustrations, but before leaving this chapter I would like to make a few observations on the subject of safety. As far as workshop practice is con-

Fig. 17   Woden Corrucut, a most useful little attachment for grooving and rebating

cerned, this can be defined as a combination of concentration, care, and common sense. All machines which are equipped with guards should have them in place at all times. I have illustrated certain tools and operations with the guards removed, purely in the interests of clarity, and the machines were not running when the photographs were taken. Any cleaning, lubricating, adjusting, and the like must be done with the tool switched off and the plug removed from its socket. In the matter of clothing, sleeves should be rolled up, ties should not be worn, and the operator should never lean over moving machinery. It is not fair to children to allow them in the workshop until they are old enough to appreciate the potential dangers. As in hand tool work, blunt tools are more likely to cause injury than sharp ones, principally by rejecting the wood and allowing the hands to be injured. If good tools are purchased and kept in proper condition, the chances of accidental injury will be greatly reduced. Power tools are not things to be feared but they must be treated with due respect.

In connection with the shaping of wood by means of electric drills and attachments it would be quite wrong to conclude without describing the extremely interesting *CeKa Zenses* system of cutters from CeKa Works, Pwllheli, North Wales. It is not possible for me within the confines of this book to do justice to this system, but I feel it highly probable that anyone who purchases one cutter and tries it out will be very impressed. The work which can be

Fig. 19   Cutting a rebate. Work must always be fed against rotation of cutter

Fig. 18   A slot cutter can be used in making combed joints for box corners

Fig. 20   A selection of CeKa Zenses cutters, with home made work table

carried out with these cutters is truly amazing and if the instruction book issued by the makers is purchased and its contents followed, a fascinating new field of woodworking will be opened up to the drill owner. As the makers say, one should not expect miracles but one can be sure of accuracy, versatility, and a great saving in time.

The cutters themselves are wood rasps but they are not made of poor quality materials. The steel used is of high quality and is case hardened so that the cutters will remain sharp for a long time. In order to use the cutters it is necessary to mount the drill in a proper pillar stand and to construct a wooden sub-table, instructions for this being given in the handbook. The setup is shown in *Figs. 18* and *19*, and as I write there are fourteen available shapes of cutter but no doubt others will be introduced in the future. Some of the range is shown in *Fig. 20*. Depth stops which can be fitted to the drill column are also available, but a small "G" cramp would provide a good alternative.

Initially it is not necessary to buy a full set of cutters since some are capable of more than one application. Best results are obtained with high speed, the minimum being 1,500 rpm

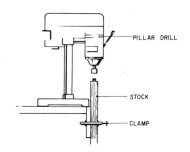

Fig. 21   Cutting a dowel on the end of a rail with a CeKa Zenses cutter

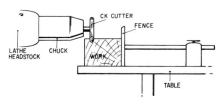

Fig. 22   Rotary cutters can be used in a lathe, with a support table for the work

under load. The higher the speed the better will be the cut and finish, and it is essential to take light cuts with a reasonable rate of feed so that the speed of the drill is not slowed too much. Working on resinous woods will tend to clog the cutters but in fairness such timbers will clog up almost anything. The application of a wire brush to the cutter while it is revolving will quickly clear them, however. They can be used on normal timbers, chipboard, plywood, and hardboard, but must not be used on metals.

The makers estimate the potential life of the cutters as between thirty and fifty working hours depending on a number of factors, and this is very good. No facilities exist for re-sharpening blunt cutters. It is important to note that unless the speed of the motor is kept high by light cuts and steady feed, there is a good chance of damaging or burning out the drill. Should this happen, it will be the fault of the operator.

No attempt should ever be made to use these cutters freehand—the drill must be mounted firmly in a drill stand. The illustrations should give a fair idea of the scope offered by these tools, and indeed it would seem that their limitations are dependent upon the ingenuity of the user.

If it is found on some woods that a poor and whiskery finish is left, this is the fault of the timber and can easily be corrected with a little abrasive paper. On most hardwoods the finish will be very good indeed. Naturally with cutters of this kind, the wood must be fed against their rotation rather than with it. Very good dowelling can be done with the appropriate cutters which will cut both the dowels and the holes to take them. It is also possible to cut dowels on the end of wood, *Fig. 21,* which gives a very strong joint. Mortices and tenons, through and stopped housings, and a wide variety of mouldings can also be produced with ease. Boards can be tongued and grooved, and chamfered at the edge of the joint, and in fact most of the normal joints used in woodwork can be made. Use can also be made of these cutters in a lathe, *Fig. 22,* which will give a higher speed than a drill, and has considerably more power. When a cutter is fitted to a drill, the shank should be inserted to its full depth.

CHAPTER 3

Universal machines

A S we have seen, the electric drill with its various aids and accessories makes a very good starting point in power woodworking, but we have many more machines to examine yet, some of them very interesting. Woodworking has the advantage of being a hobby which can be profitable as well as interesting and it seems that many men retiring from business take it up and become very keen. To others it is a sideline, and they are perhaps making furniture or toys to augment their income. Whatever the reason for wanting to set up a workshop, the moment comes when the decision has to be taken as to whether there are to be a number of individual tools, arranged to cover the type of work which is envisaged, or whether there should be a universal machine which will do virtually all that is likely to be required.

It must be pointed out in the first instance that a machine which has been carefully designed to do a given job will usually be far more efficient at that job than the corresponding part of a universal. The choice, however, is not as simple as that. To have a machine for each job means a separate motor for each machine, which will put the costs up dramatically to start with. There is also the question of space, because it is certainly not safe to work in a shop which is crowded with machines—

Fig. 1 Emco Star universal woodworking machine with Emco Rex planer attached. From Burgess Power Tools Ltd

Fig. 2 **A general view of the Coronet Major Universal, with head-stock partly swung round**

each one should have at least eight feet clear working space all round it. If it happens that the number of machine operations you are likely to need to do is fairly small and you have the space and the cash to go for individual machines, then this is likely to be the best course to adopt, but you will need to study the market carefully before making too many hasty decisions.

The universal, on the other hand, is well worth thinking about because a number of machines grouped on a single power unit can be very effective. Points to watch when buying a universal are that it should be robust and capable of standing up to the job, and that spare parts and accessories can be obtained with ease. Some of the universal machines I have seen had too much money spent on making them look attractive, whereas it would have been far better used to make them stronger or more versatile.

Universals are usually based either on a lathe or on a sawbench, and if you do not want to do any wood-

turning a saw-based machine will do quite well, although there are some advantages in having the lathe bed apart from its obvious use, as we will see. *Figs. 1* and *2* show typical universal machines.

The range of these tools is quite large and we cannot go through each one in detail, but we will look at the two main lathe-based tools, the *Coronet* and the *Myford ML8*; also the *Burgess Emco Star*, which is a very different tool. The radial arm saw will be examined in another chapter, and this in a sense can be regarded as a universal tool since it will perform many functions apart from sawing, with the necessary attachments. The *Myford ML8* is a very popular tool, and a unit built up of lathe, sawbench, planer, and mortiser, with perhaps a sander and drill chuck, is capable of a wide range of woodworking operations.

A similar unit can be built up in the *Coronet* range, and this is one good point about this sort of machine— one does not have to buy everything all at once. The starting point can be simply a lathe with motor if desired and the other items added later. I have shown both the *Coronet* and *Myford* machines in the illustrations, and they are similar in operation, so let us consider the *Coronet Major* as an example.

· This, like the *Myford*, has a lathe bed with head and tailstocks, and a cabinet stand can be purchased for mounting it. This is by no means essential since the tool could be mounted on solid trestles and used to make its own wooden cabinet. This would allow the inclusion of drawers and cupboards in which the smaller accessories, cutters, and so forth could be kept. There is one other point in favour of building one's own cabinet, that being the question of the actual working height of the machine. The factory-made cabinets are all the same size, which is more than can be said for the users, and if you intend to use the tool for woodturning the centres should be at elbow height when you are standing comfortably upright. If the machine is mounted much lower than

this you are in for some very unpleasant backaches.

These lathes are very good indeed. I have used both makes and would recommend either. They are far removed from toys, being really sturdy and solid and capable of handling quite heavy turning jobs with ease. It is said that a little learning is a dangerous thing, and this applies very much in the case of woodturning. I shall not therefore go into any details whatsoever in this book, but those who are interested may like to read "Modern Woodturning", which I wrote recently, and which deals with the subject exhaustively.

Logically, the first attachment to be bought for the machine will be the sawbench. This will have to take a lot of punishment in the course of its life, so it should be a good solid table, cast and machined rather than pressed out. On tools of this sort the sawbench is made to rise and fall and to tilt when necessary. The rise and fall spindle type will be discussed later, but it is not possible to in-

Fig. 3   Rise and fall of Coronet Major sawtable is operated by rack and pinion gearing

**Fig. 4   Planing
attachment for
Coronet machines
(guard removed)**

corporate it into this sort of machine, since the spindle is essentially a part of the lathe.

The table illustrated has a rack and pinion mechanism for the rise and fall, with a clamping lever to hold it in any selected position, *Fig. 3*. The saw itself has a groove to take the mitre guide to the left of the blade, the latter being 10 in. in diameter and giving a full 3 in. depth of cut. This is likely to be plenty for the average home user, since he can handle wood 6 in. thick by turning it over for a second cut. There is a removable metal insert round the blade which can be removed from the table when a moulding cutter head is used, or when a wobble or drunken saw is used, as we shall see.

The power unit for this machine is a *Brook Gryphon* one horsepower motor, which can be supplied in single or three phrase as required. These motors are brushless and do not interfere in any way with radio or television. They are also totally enclosed, and therefore do not suffer from the effects of dust. Drive is taken through a three-stepped pulley block with vee belt, and for normal

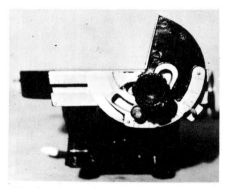

**Fig. 5   Front view of planer, showing
clamp knob which holds fence in
selected position**

sawing purposes the centre pulleys should be used, giving approximately 3,000 rpm.

The planer, *Fig. 4,* is a useful little tool with a 4½ in. cutter block. The motor is double ended, the planer drive being taken from a pulley at the opposite end to the main drive, giving 6,000 rpm at the cutter block. Since the block carries two blades there is a running speed of 12,000 cuts per minute, which is the optimum for this sort of planer. Provided the wood is fed correctly to the tool and at a reasonable speed the finish produced is very good. The planer is equipped with a fence which can be tilted to 45 degrees one way and 5 degrees the other, though this can be reversed if so desired by moving the setting pin into another hole. There is a graduated scale on the front end of the planer, *Fig. 7*, which allows tilt settings to be made but before it is used, the fence should be set at 90 degrees to the table by means of a square, and the marker on the calibrated scale set to zero. The fence itself has a clamping knob at the front and can be moved across the table to any selected position and locked there.

Another very useful feature of this sort of planer is that it can rebate down to $\frac{1}{2}$ in. in depth, and up to the width of the cutter block, but if a wide rebate is made it should be done in several passes, lowering the table a little more each time. If too much wood is taken out at once there is a grave danger that the workpiece may be kicked back, and the operator's fingers may find their way into the cutters. If an angled rebate is required, as perhaps in the case of a window cill, it can be done quite simply by tilting the planer fence.

In *Fig. 6* the planer is shown with its thicknessing attachment fitted. This does not take long to put on and is surprisingly effective and accurate in use, but it is important to note that the front table of the planer must be lowered to the maximum before the thicknesser can be used. Timber to be thicknessed should first be planed on two adjacent sides so that they are square; these planed sides are then placed face up on the planer table as the wood goes through.

Apart from its obvious value in bringing a quantity of wood up square and to the same thickness this attachment is a safety feature, since it is virtually impossible to cut your hands while it is in place unless you really try! It helps also in the handling of long boards, which can be pushed through so far and pulled the rest of the way. There are, as we shall see, planers of what is known as the 'over and under' variety, which means that wood is planed over the blades in the normal manner, but for thicknessing it is fed back underneath the cutter block, and is taken through by the machine automatically. Most of the small planers such as the ones we have been discussing can have extensions to either front or back tables or to both, which can be a big help when handling long material alone.

Another very important item for machines such as these universals which I have mentioned is the mortising attachment, which can be used with either hollow square chisels, or the slot miller bits, *Fig. 7*, which are much faster cutting but leave a rounded end to the mortice. This is no real problem since it can be squared off in a moment with a sharp chisel but I do not bother to do this as I find it easier to round over the edges of the tenon with a rasp or on a disc sander. There is less strain on the machine with this type and as they require no special setting and very little attention, they are becoming popular.

Fig. 6 Thicknessing attachment in position on planer

Fig. 7 Slot miller bit and chuck mounted on Coronet Major

One of these mortisers is shown in *Fig. 8*. It has stops to limit the lateral travel of its table and the forward travel, so that the length and depth of the mortice can be set exactly with very little trouble.

There is also provision for the rise and fall of the table, to allow the cutter to be centred to the wood as necessary. Usually machines of this type have an auxiliary table, which can be purchased if required, and this has a number of uses as the illustrations show. It makes a fine sanding table for use with a disc sander, and it has a fence which can be fitted in two positions, either parallel to the lathe bed or at 90 degrees to it, so that it can be used for dowelling with a suitable drill held in a Jacobs chuck in the headstock.

At the moment I am simply running through the main features of these

Fig. 8 Mortiser on Coronet machine in use. Note use of scrap wood to protect work

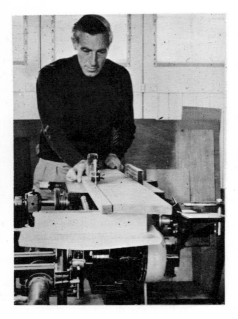

Another useful machine which we will examine in more detail later on is the *Emco Star*, from *Burgess Power Tools*. It is an Austrian machine, and is very cleverly thought out. The basis of the tool, as you can see, is a unit combining two saws, a circular and a bandsaw. The tool can be tilted from one position to the other, according to which saw is to be used, and a safety device is built in so that changing over from one saw to another disconnects the drive to the one which is not in use. The importance of this from a safety viewpoint is obvious. *Figs. 1, 10* and *11* give a reasonably clear idea of what the tool is all about, and there is a useful

machines, and we will go into the real details of all their facilities later. Since the complete headstock of the *Coronet* machine can be swung round as shown in *Fig. 9,* the ripping of long planks is very much simplified, there being a roller on top of the table fence over which the timber rides.

There are numerous other devices which can be attached to these machines such as belt sanders, grindstones, and so on. They are very robust and represent excellent value for money since with proper care they should last a lifetime.

Fig. 10 Bandsaw of Burgess Emco Star cuts hard and soft woods with ease

little belt sander and a disc sander with table, so we have two saws and two sanders which can be used without any changing of parts or hunting for spanners. The *Emco Rex* planer, which is of the over and under type can be fitted to the machine as the

Fig. 11 Jig saw attachment in use with Emco Star. Note support roller behind blade, and foot which holds work down to table

Figs. 12 and 13 Coronet woodworking machine shown with planer and belt sander (left). The same machine can also be fitted up for woodturning (right). Other attachments can be fitted

illustrations show, and it is a really good tool.

Attachments for the *Emco Star* include a fretsaw and a jigsaw, both of which are most efficient, and changing over to them takes very little time. With the addition of tool rests, etc., it is possible to do woodturning. Two speeds are available through the switch control, these being 1,500 and 3,000 rpm.

Other machines of the sawbench-based type are available, and in fact there are quite a number. Examples are the *Inca*, the *Signal*, the *Dominion*, and the *Coronet International*.

The last is a fairly recent introduction, and is an interesting machine for several reasons. Basically it is a large and solid sawbench with a rise and fall spindle and a tilting arbor. The *Coronet Capitol* planer can be fitted on the left, and on the right hand side of the cabinet there is a headstock identical to that used on the *Major* lathe. This headstock can only be used when the sawblade is in its normal vertical position, but it is of great interest in that a bar similar to the *Major* bed bar can be attached to the machine, and all the

attachments which fit the *Major* can then be used.

The other important feature of the tool is that it has a fully variable speed which can be altered while the motor is running, and instead of bogging the user down with a lot of facts and figures relating to speeds in rpm, there is a panel on the front of the cabinet showing exactly where the speed change lever should be placed for any given operation. It is a heavy tool and not the sort of thing one would want to move about very often, but against this there is the fact that it is robust. A thicknessing attachment is available for the *Capitol* planer as an extra, see *Fig. 6,* which shows it in position.

So far we have been generalising about tools, but now we can get down to seeing how some of them behave in use, looking for their good and bad points, and arriving at the real object of the book, which is to go through the range of power tools and see what can be done with them with a little ingenuity.

CHAPTER 4

Power planing

PLANING timber by hand is one of the most satisfying jobs in the woodworker's trade, and if he has the skill to sharpen, set, and use the planes as they should be used, he will derive great pleasure from watching those beautiful shavings curl back as the tool moves along.

Fig. 1   Burgess Emco Rex B20 10 in. × 5 in. planer being used to prepare stock for a house name plate

Unfortunately this is a slow process, and the man who is engaged in any form of commercial woodworking, or who uses timber for jobs around his home which have to be done in the least possible time, must soon discover that he needs a machine planer. Having once had one in his workshop, he will never want to be without it.

Timber can of course be purchased ready planed and for some jobs, particularly where wide boards are needed this is a good idea, but where precision is called for there are problems. Frequently you will find that a batch of timber bought as 2 in. by 1 in. planed, just as an example, varies in thickness through the batch since it may not have been planed all at the same time, and one man's idea of a setting may not agree with that of his colleague.

Another problem arises in that although the wood may have left the machine straight and true, exposure to sun and wind are quite likely to have warped and twisted it since. In my experience you will be lucky if this is not the case. This sort of thing can be most frustrating, especially where joints have to be cut. There are easy ways to cut joints on a sawbench with which we will deal in due course, but mostly these rely on all the wood being exactly the same thickness.

A man who owns a circular saw can buy his timber in larger sections and cut it to size as it is needed, passing it over the planer as soon as it is cut. This has obvious advantages in that you do not suddenly run out of a given dimension of timber—it can always be cut as it is needed.

Planers come into two categories, these being the jointer or surface planer, to which an attachment can usually be fitted for thicknessing; and the planer/thicknesser, which is a more expensive tool, though it is more efficient. *Fig. 1* shows one of the latter variety, the *Burgess B20*, which has a ten inch cutter block with two knives. This is a lovely machine to use and is of the over and under type, timber to be thicknessed being passed through below the cutter block, with its planed side downwards, *Fig. 2*. A small jointer with a $4\frac{1}{2}$ in. cutter block is shown in *Fig. 3*, this tool being made for the *Coronet* universals.

Machine planers, when properly set up and used will give an excellent surface. One has the big advantage that once the machine has been set and the cut tested on a piece of scrap, of being able to plane a pile of material very quickly and with complete accuracy. There is no need to check each piece for squareness.

The basic principles of power planers are not difficult to grasp even if you have never seen one. The heart of the tool is the cutter block, which can rotate at a fixed speed. The actual speed of rotation is dictated by the number of cutters in the block, since the optimum cutting speed is 12,000 cuts per minute. You will see, therefore, that with two blades the speed must be 6,000 rpm, with three blades 4,000, and with four blades 3,000. Two-bladed blocks tend to be the best, because of the difficulty of getting all the blade edges set in exactly the same plane. (No pun intended!) With the two-bladed block, if one knife is set a fraction higher than the other, there will still be 6,000 effective cuts per minute, but one high blade on a three-bladed

Fig. 2   Emco Rex B20 power-fed thicknessing unit in use on a wide board

Fig. 3   A 4½-inch planer, attachment to the Coronet Major. Note tilting fence

block means 4,000 cuts, and one high blade on a four-bladed machine will give only 3,000. Theoretically, a four-bladed block should give a better finish than a two-bladed one, all else being equal, but in practice this is rarely the case. From a user's point of view, the two-bladed block means far less trouble when it comes to setting up and sharpening, and on an overall basis there is less expense involved. *Figs. 4, 5,* and *6* with their captions will help quite a lot to clarify these matters.

When a new planer leaves the factory it will have been ground, set, and honed ready for use. After a time, however, the knives will become dull and need attention. This will be obvious to the user because he will notice that the machine has become noisier when cutting, and it will be progressively more difficult to hold the wood down to the knives.

When this happens, attention should be given to the blades at once. They should be examined to ensure that no chipping of the edges has occurred, and if it has, the blades should be changed and the faulty ones returned to the factory to be reground. If there is no chipping the blades can be honed in position, using the following method. It is essential for accurate planing that the rear, or take-off, table of the machine should be at a tangent to the cutting circle of the knives, and this can be checked by taking a piece of scrap wood which has been planed true along one edge, rubbing this edge with chalk, and placing it on the rear table overhanging the cutter block as shown in

Fig. 4   Using a piece of wood to set planer knives. Edge of wood has been planed true and rubbed with chalk

Fig. 5   Knives being set by means of a batten with two pencil marks

Fig. 4.

This operation, like any other adjustment to power tools, must be done with the plug removed from the mains and not just with the machine switched off. If the cutter block is now rotated in its normal direction by hand the knives should ideally disturb the chalk without moving the wood. If you can adjust them like this, they will be right.

Another method which is sometimes advocated is the making of two marks on the edge of a piece of wood, $\frac{1}{8}$ in. apart. The wood is then placed on the rear table so that the front mark lines up with the edge of it, *Fig. 5*. If the block is now revolved by hand, the blade should carry the wood forward so that the second mark aligns with the table edge. I cannot entirely agree with this, because it obviously puts the knives above the surface of the rear table, whereas they should be exactly level with it. Whichever method is adopted, however, it is essential to check the knives at each end and in the centre.

To hone the blades while they are still in the cutter block one lowers the front, or feed, table so that a small oilstone (with a paper wrapper to protect the table surface but leaving $\frac{1}{2}$ in. or so of stone uncovered) can be laid on this table and will lie flat across the bevel of the knife, *Fig. 6*. Holding the driving pulley of the planer with one hand, the oilstone is run back and forth across the blade. It is as well to stop after a few strokes to wipe the blade and make sure that the stone is cutting right

Fig. 6   Blades are honed in the block. Note use of paper to protect the table

across the bevel. Any alteration to the angle of this bevel will destroy the efficiency of the planer. It is possible to regrind planer knives in the home workshop but I would not really advise it, unless you are an expert in metal work. The cost of regrinding at the factory is negligible anyway, so all you need is a spare pair of blades.

Assuming all the settings to be correct, the use of the planer is quite straightforward and once the tool has been used a few times it will present no problems. Here, however, I must warn the new owner of a power planer against any nonchalance or carelessness. These tools are statistically more dangerous than circular saws, and they must at all times be used with care and common sense.

Let us get on with using the planer, so that we can find out how it really works. You can see by the illustrations that there are two completely separate tables, the feed, or front table, and the taking off, or rear table. On some machines it will be found that both tables can be raised and lowered, but in the normal way of things it is only the front table which we adjust. The height of this table sets the depth of cut. In other words, if both tables are at the same height, wood passed across the machine will not be cut at all, assuming the rear table to be correctly set. Lower the front table by $\frac{1}{16}$ in., and the machine will give that depth of cut. This can be seen in *Fig. 7*.

Some very small planers have a maximum depth of cut of $\frac{1}{8}$ in., but

Fig. 7 **Showing how depth of cut as difference in height between the two tables**

if more than about $\frac{1}{16}$ in. is taken, the finish will be poor. With larger planers, however, it may be possible for purposes of rebating to take out as much as half an inch. For normal planing, then, about $\frac{1}{16}$ in. will be adequate and should leave a good finish on the work. In order to bring some timber up dead square, we first check the planer fence to see that it is at 90 degrees to the table using a square, as in *Fig. 8*. When this has been established it is a good idea to check that the calibration pointer under the front table is at zero.

Fig. 8 **Checking planer fence for squareness with table**

Fig. 9 Taking first cut
on rough piece of
wood

Fig. 10 Note
projection of ends of
blades, to give clean
corners when rebating

The tool is now set to take off $\frac{1}{16}$ in. or so, and one side of the wood is passed over the cutters, *Fig. 9*. This planed side is now put up against the fence and kept in full contact with it while the second side is planed. If the wood is out of square it may be necessary to pass the second side over the knives more than once until it is being cut right across the surface. This process will be repeated until all four faces of the wood have been dealt with. A check with a square now should show that the timber is true, and if it is not it means that the wood was not held correctly to the fence all the time. A little practice will soon put matters right, so do not despair.

If you examine carefully the way in which the knives are set in the block on smaller planers which are designed to cut rebates, you will see that they project a little on the left hand side, *Fig. 10*. This projection is most important if a clean cut is to be obtained in a rebate, and if the knives are changed at any time it must not be overlooked. My own method of setting knives in planers is with a dial gauge, which is extremely accurate, but I only do it because someone was kind enough to give me the instrument.

The method of holding the knives in the block varies with different makes. On the *Coronet* planers there is a slot in each knife, and a screw at each end with a fixed collar to fit into the slot. This is a very good arrangement, since one has only to loosen the Allen screws which clamp the knives in place and they can be raised or lowered with micrometer precision by turning the screws, which obviously moves the knives up or down in the block.

Some planers do not have this sort of arrangement and a very good idea with these is to use a large magnet, like the ones which were once used in motor car magnetos. If one of these is laid on the rear table, the knife can be loosened and brought up so that at its highest point it is held by the magnet, *Fig. 11.* The important thing here is that this type of horseshoe magnet holds each end of the knife at the same height. The screws can then be tightened and the setting should be correct.

This setting of the knives to the rear table is critical, and for that reason it is best not to move the rear table unless you have to. If the setting is right, wood can be passed over the cutters neatly on to the rear table. If, however, the rear table is too high the wood will catch on its edge, whereas if it is too low there will be a gap between the table and the wood. It is worth bearing in mind that timber in store is often stood on end and so there may be dirt and grit

embedded in the ends of the planks. The life of the cutters will be extended if the ends of the planks are cut off before planing commences. It is also unwise to take too light a cut on old or dirty timber; $\frac{1}{8}$ in. will be in order, taking the edges of the knives well below the dirt.

The planing of short pieces of wood presents some problems, and can be dangerous under certain circumstances. It is not advisable to attempt to plane wood less than 6 in. long, and anything of this nature should be handled with the aid of a pusher block, which can be made quite easily in the workshop, *Fig. 12.* One of the biggest dangers with power planers is the kick-back, or rapid rejection of the wood by the cutters,

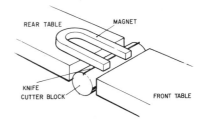

Fig. 11 Setting planer knives with a magnet. Tighten securing screws while bevel of cutter is flat against magnet

Fig. 12 Home made pusher block for safety in planing

and there is no real need for this to occur. The causes of it are traceable either to blunt knives, too fast a feed rate, or both. As with the portable or drill-driven saw, do not overload by taking too deep a cut or feeding too fast, or your cutting speed will drop and the finish will be poor. Planers do have guards and for obvious reasons these should be used but I have had to take them off in some of the illustrations for the sake of clarity. When there is a lot of edging to be done on thin material, the fence should be moved across the table from time to time or all the wear will take place at one point on the cutters, which is not a good thing.

One of the most important principles involved in the use of a machine planer is that the left hand presses the timber down on to the rear table, while the right hand does not press down, it simply feeds forward. The truth of the cut comes from the rear table, not from the front one. It seems hardly worth saying, but wood should always be fed to the cutters the right way of the

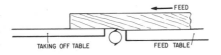

Fig. 13 Planing must be done with the direction of grain where possible

grain, *Fig. 13*, just as hand planing is done with the grain, and if you do not observe this the finish will suffer.

For the sake of safety it is as well to get into a definite way of using the planer and to stick to it as far as possible. The recommended pro-

cedure for surface planing is to feed the wood forward with both hands on the front table, until sufficient wood has passed over the knives to allow the left hand to be taken round to press it down on to the rear table. As the last few inches of wood approach the cutters, the right hand is taken round to join it, so that the cut finishes with both hands over the rear table, neither having passed directly over the cutters. With this, or any other powered cutting tool, familiarity must not be allowed to breed contempt.

With small planers such as the *Myford* and *Coronet* it is possible to cut very accurate rebates up to the width of the cutters, and down as deep as $\frac{1}{2}$ in. in some cases. A rebate $\frac{1}{2}$ in. deep can be taken in one pass if it is up to 1 in. wide, but the wider the rebate the more necessary it will be to remove the wood in several passes increasing the depth each time. If this is not done, there is every chance of a nasty kick-back. Rebating is done by setting the planer fence to give the required width, and lowering the front table to give the exact depth, as in *Fig. 14*. It is always best to try this out on a piece of scrap wood and measure it before going on with the job in hand. The wood is then passed steadily over the cutters, and a smooth, dead square rebate should result (*Fig. 15*).

Some glazing bar is shown in *Figs. 16* to *18*, suitable for greenhouses or garden frames, which can be made very simply on a planer of this type. The method is to take out the two rebates first, *Fig. 17*, then to tilt the

Fig. 14   Rebating in softwood on Coronet planer. Hardwoods are handled equally well .

Fig. 15   Work being rebated is held firmly and fed slowly to the cutters

Fig. 16   Simple glazing bar made on the planer

Fig. 17   Two rebates are made, then front edges are chamfered with planer fence tilted

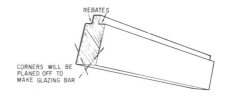

REBATES

CORNERS WILL BE PLANED OFF TO MAKE GLAZING BAR

Fig. 18   Edges of glazing bar being chamfered. Note batten clamped on table to support work

planer fence and nip off the front edges of the wood. If you feel nervous about this in case the wood should slide sideways on the table while being chamfered, a piece of batten can be fixed to the planer table as shown in *Fig. 18*. If this is fed over the planer so that it runs the length of the machine, it can be clamped in place and will effectively support the wood, so making the operation considerably safer.

This type of planer usually has a thicknessing attachment, the *Coronet* version being shown in *Ch. 3, Fig. 6*.

As you can see, it is in the form of an arch which fits over the planer, and it is held by two bolts. There is a thicknessing plate which can be raised or lowered and clamped in any desired position. There is also a plate carrying two strong steel springs which hold the wood up against the thicknessing plate as it is pushed through. The front table is lowered as far as it will go when using the thicknesser, except when very heavy timber is being thicknessed which might cause the springs to bend. In such cases it is wise to raise the front table a little, to give the springs more purchase.

Another operation which can be performed on a small planer with rebating facilities is the cutting of tenons, the proviso here being that the wood is all of equal thickness. Tenoning in this way is no more than end-rebating in effect, and some large planers have tenoning facilities built in, with a sliding table on the left hand side to which the wood can be clamped. In these tools small

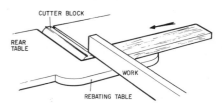

Fig. 19   Using a board to feed wood sideways in work like tenoning to keep the wood square to the fence

cutters are provided which cut across the grain at the tenon shoulder so that the finish is smooth. With planers of the type we are discussing there are no such provisions, so we have two problems, one being to hold the wood square to the cutter block, and the other that we must cut across the grain with a scribing gauge or knife blade before starting operations.

A jig made up as in *Fig. 19* will help us to feed the wood square, and it will also help to prevent spelching, or breaking away, where the cutters emerge.

The planer is a useful machine for tapering wood, as in the making of furniture legs for example. This can be done very well provided the essential principles are clearly understood. *Fig. 20* will help to make it clear, but this happens to be one of those jobs which sounds complicated when described, yet is, in fact, simplicity itself once it has been done a time or two. The wood used for operations of this sort must first be prepared perfectly square. There are two points to consider here, one being the tapering of a piece of wood which is shorter than the front table of the planer, and the other what happens when the wood is

Fig. 20 Starting the taper cut

longer than the table.

Let us take first of all the case of a piece of wood shorter than the planer table. In the first place it is obvious that the taper cannot start right at the extreme end of the wood or it will go straight into the cutters, so the timber is prepared a fraction longer than required, and cut to true length after tapering. The cut, therefore, must start a short distance along the wood, so that the latter can be rested on the rear table. I normally make a pencil mark on the planer fence and the table so that I can put each piece down in the same spot. When the wood is lowered on to the cutters there will be a very slight kick, but as long as the workpiece is firmly held, all will be well. If you are fainthearted you can put a wooden stop block on a strip of wood and attach it to the planer fence. This will serve the double purpose of preventing kicks and locating all pieces in the same starting position.

The depth of cut of the planer is set to the amount we want taken off at the end of the leg (which may be a quarter of an inch) and the wood is placed against the stop block, lowered on to the rear table and fed gently forward. A push stick should always be used for this operation, and remember that as the cut progresses so the depth increases; attention must therefore be paid to the rate of feed. Each side is treated in the same way, and we have a neatly tapered leg.

So far so good, but what if the leg is longer than the planer table, which is quite likely? In such a case, the part to be tapered is divided into two, and if the taper needed is $\frac{1}{4}$ in., the planer is set to $\frac{1}{8}$ in., and all four sides are tapered from the centre mark. When this has been done, the table is set down a further $\frac{1}{8}$ in., and the material tapered on all four sides again from the top mark. It may sound involved but it is not really so bad. On a longer piece it may be necessary to divide the work into three, and go through the process three times, with three separate depth settings.

In *Fig. 21* you can see a furniture

Fig. 21   Tapered leg
with tapered foot. The
whole job is done
entirely on the planer

Figs. 22 and 23   If the
work is lifted off
before the end of each
cut, a foot is left,
which can be tapered
or left square. Note
mark on table of
planer, to which the
end of work is taken

leg which has been tapered by the methods outlined above but a foot has been left at the bottom, and this in its turn has been tapered. This is quite effective and easy to do. If a mark is made on the table or fence at the right point, the wood can be lifted off the cutters when its end is level with it. When all sides have been done, a foot is left, *Figs. 22* and *23*.

The tapering of the foot itself is done by setting the table to the required depth, and drawing the foot up over the knives. A piece of scrap wood on the rear table helps to keep the cut straight. The turner may like to centre this in his lathe and turn the whole leg, which comes out very well. Usually it will be found that the wood is a little rough where the cut was stopped, but some attention with abrasive paper will soon correct this.

Cutting bevels and chamfers on a planer is an easy job if tackled in the right way. For the benefit of anyone who may not be sure of the

Fig. 24 Showing difference between bevel and chamfer

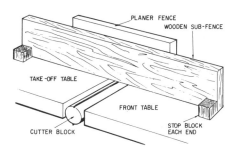

Fig. 25 Use of board with stop blocks when chamfering

difference, a bevel is an angled cut which joins two opposite sides of a piece of wood, whereas a chamfer joins two adjacent sides, *Fig. 24*. All that is needed to perform these operations is the tilting of the fence to the appropriate angle, and the setting of the depth to give the required cut. It may be found helpful to have a piece of wood across the planer tables as a guide to keep the workpiece up to the fence.

Ordinary chamfers are no problem, but as I mentioned earlier, on many small planers both tables can be lowered and this becomes necessary in order to produce stopped chamfers, *Fig. 25*. I try to avoid this because it means setting the rear table back after the job is done, but this is just laziness. Stopped chamfers are cut by lowering both tables by the same amount, and it is advisable to fix a wooden fence on to the planer fence with stop blocks screwed to it

at the requisite points. The distance between these will regulate the length of the cut. With the fence tilted by the required amount, normally 45 degrees, the wood is placed against the rear stop block, lowered on to the cutters, and fed forward until it reaches the other stop, when it is lifted clear.

For those whose woodturning has not reached a very high standard, the planer can be useful in removing the corners of square lengths of wood before they go into the lathe, but the centres should be marked first. This is not really a necessary practice, but beginners feel more confident when the corners have been taken off.

Figs. 1 and *2* show the *Emco Rex B20* planing and thicknessing machine which is a most sophisticated piece of equipment. It has a double-bladed cutter block, and it is a really first class job. It is perhaps a little more than the average home handyman would need, but there is no doubt that anyone who can get hold of one and use it for a while will be spoilt for anything else. A stand is available for the planer, as shown in the illustrations, but this is not essential as one can build a wooden stand for it quite easily.

For normal planing the depth of cut is set by the small knurled handle, *Fig. 26*, and there is a scale provided to indicate the depth selected. The fence is of wood, and can be tilted either way. The guard is in sections which are hinged to each other so that as much of the cutter block as is needed may be uncovered.

As a planer for work up to 10 in.

in width this is a really good tool, but naturally it is very important to see that the cutters are kept razor sharp. It is when used for thicknessing that it really excels. As with all thicknessers, two adjacent sides of

Fig. 26 Adjusting depth of cut on Burgess B20 planer. Control is conveniently placed at front of feed table

Fig. 27 Underside of B20 planer, showing the anti-kick-back fingers which prevent rejection of wood during thicknessing

the work should be planed over the tables in the normal way, the work then being fed through the thicknesser, in this case with the planed sides downwards so that the uncut sides face up to the cutter block. With an overhead thicknessing attachment, such as the *Coronet*, the planed sides would be put through upwards so that the unplaned sides face down to the cutter block. The *B20* feeds the work through automatically at the correct speed, and the finish is very good.

No attempt should ever be made with tools of this type to remove shavings from the thicknessing table while the motor is running; the thought of a hand becoming involved with a feed roller is not pleasant! Work being fed through the thicknessing part of this machine cannot be kicked back at the operator because there are anti-kick-back fingers fitted to prevent this from happening.

The accuracy of these thicknessers is quite remarkable, and it is perfectly possible to make pieces of veneer for repairing furniture and such jobs, because one can thickness down to $\frac{1}{32}$ in. I have put ordinary hardboard through thicknessers at exhibitions and rolled it up like a film afterwards, which always seems to fascinate onlookers. It has a practical application as well in that strips of hardboard thicknessed like this can be used as edging strips on man-made boards, and when the job is sanded and painted it has a first class appearance.

A point worth noting is that when a board has to be planed all round

Fig. 28 Useful electric hand planer from Wolf tools.

Fig. 29 Rebating with a Bosch hand planer, using auxiliary fence.

on its edges it is unsatisfactory to pass the end grain straight across the cutters. In order to prevent the wood from breaking away at the end of the cut it is fed over the cutters for an inch or so, then reversed and fed across until the second cut meets the first.

In *Figs. 28* and *29* I have shown two portable electric planes. These are very useful for on-site work, or any application where it is necessary to take the tool to the job rather than the other way about. It should be borne in mind that these tools are meant for removing wood quickly and not so much for finishing a surface. Widths vary, and the tools give a good finish if the material being planed is narrower than the cutters, but when used on a wide surface they do leave marks which have to be dealt with by sanding. Setting of depth of cut is similar to the setting of a bench planer, in that there is what amounts to a front and a rear table, the depth of cut being varied by altering the setting of the front one.

Usually the makers supply an oilstone and a jig of some kind so that the cutters can be removed and honed with accuracy. As with bigger planes, the cutters must be set so that they are level with the rear table, or the back half of the sole if you prefer that description. These are useful tools for levelling rough timber or for shooting the bottoms of doors.

CHAPTER 5

Circular saws and sawbenches

ARLIER in the book we had a look at portable circular saws and drill-driven attachments, but now we have arrived at the point where we should discuss the sawbench as such, which is a very different matter. Circular saws seem to strike terror into the hearts of some people, and I have never really understood this. One is after all in far more danger when crossing a busy street or driving one's car than when using such a tool with intelligence and common sense. Once a man has installed a circular saw and bench in his workshop and become accustomed to it, he will be unable to imagine how he managed before it arrived.

There are, of course, good sawbenches and bad ones, and my sincere advice to anyone who is contemplating the purchase of one is to wait until he can afford to buy a really good one from a maker who has a reputation to uphold. Cheap sawbenches are quite definitely a false economy, but a good one is a tool for life. In fact the sawbenches which are fitted to some of the universal machines are excellent in quality, and

capable of really good work.

For the home user, a 7 in. or 8 in. blade giving a 2 in. depth of cut will often suffice, or a 10 in. blade, giving a 3 in. cut.

It is definitely best to buy a bench which has a cast and machined table rather than an alloy pressing. The latter is suitable for rough general work, but if it is intended to do cabinet making or other precision work, the table is most important. There should be a slot for the slide of the mitre gauge on one side of the blade at least, and there should be a good strong rip fence, preferably extending right across the table. If this is capable of being clamped at the back as well as at the front, so much the better, though it is not essential. Sawbenches which have static tables and facilities for rise and fall and tilt of the blade itself are expensive, and it is not vital to go for one of these. The type where the table itself rises and falls and can be made to tilt will do equally well for almost every job. It is an advantage if the rip fence has rough adjustment by means of a slide on its mounting bar, and a fine micrometer type

**Fig. 1   Coarse adjust-
ment clamping lever
for rip fence**

adjustment as well, *Fig. 1*. *Figs. 9*
and *10* show typical sawbenches of a
useful type.

The guard is an important part of the
set-up and should be used wherever
possible. I say this because there are
occasions when it cannot be used.
Many guards nowadays are mounted
on the riving knife, *Fig. 2*, and since
this has to be removed for all cutting
where the blade does not pass right
through the wood, the guard must
come off as well. In some cases the
guard is mounted on an arm secured
to the side of the sawtable, but here
again it can be an obstruction when
crosscutting.

When you receive your new sawbench, there are some checks which
must be carried out before it is put to
use. It will have left the factory in
good condition and properly set, but
things can sometimes be knocked
out of true in transit and unless all
the settings are as they should be, the
saw will give trouble. In many cases
the nut which holds the sawblade in
place has a lefthand thread, so that

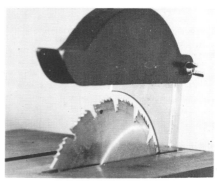

**Fig. 2   Riving knife mounted im-
mediately behind the saw blade, keeps
kerf from closing on back of blade**

it is self-tightening in use. If the blade
is fitted at the righthand end of the
spindle the thread will be a normal
one, but always make sure that this
nut is securely tightened.

My own methods of setting up
and checking a sawtable do not seem
to agree with everyone else's, but it
certainly seems that they work, so I
will give them here. The rip fence
should be brought over to the edge
of the mitre gauge slot, *Fig. 3*, to
check that it is truly parallel. Near

Fig. 3   Rip fence must
be parallel to mitre
gauge slot

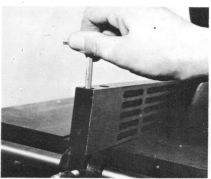

Fig. 4   Adjusting rip fence parallel to
the mitre gauge slot

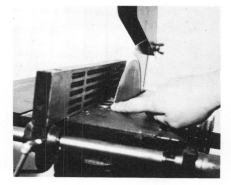

Fig. 5   Using a coin between rip fence
and blade to check that no discrepancy
exists

enough will not do at all, it has to be
in perfect alignment. If you find it is
out of true, which is quite likely, then
it must be adjusted until it is correct,
Fig. 4. Once this has been done, the
rip fence is moved over towards the
blade and a coin or washer placed
between the two so that it touches
both saw and fence at the front of the
blade, *Fig. 5*, but not so tightly that
it will not slide. The coin can now be
slid from front to back of the saw-

blade, and if all is well it will maintain contact with both blade and
fence all the way. If it jams or leaves
a gap, then the table is out of line.
Again, adjustment is called for, and
it is no use trying to use the machine
until you have this exactly right.

A final check after this is to lower
the table to its full extent and stand
a try square on the surface to check
that the angle between table and
blade is ninety degrees. If it is, the

Fig. 6 Tilt indicator
being set and locked
by retaining screw

tilt indicator can be set to zero, *Fig. 6*, and all may be well, but then again it may not. This rather depends on the quality of the blade itself.

A good quality blade will cut true, but a cheap thin one should be disposed of, or it will always be a nuisance by whipping in the cut and leaving a wavy surface. There are numerous types of sawblade available for various purposes, but you are likely to find that your machine has been fitted with what is known as a "combination" blade. This is a type of general purpose blade which will both rip and crosscut fairly efficiently, but will not perform either function as well as a blade which was designed for that specific purpose. The home user does not really need to get bogged down in peripheral speeds, pulley sizes, and so forth unless he intends to build his own sawbench, which is a subject I shall not deal with here. What he needs is a bench which has been motorised with a motor giving sufficient power

and running at the right speed.

Other blades for which he may find uses are the thin-rimmed plywood blade which, as its name implies, is thinner at the rim than at the centre and is designed for the cutting of materials such as plywood, where little depth is involved. The planer blade is another useful saw, having no set, and is intended for crosscutting where the smoothest possible finish is needed. It should not be used for ripping. Other items such as wobble saws and moulding heads can be fitted to sawbenches, but we will deal with them later.

For the moment let us consider the use of the sawbench in its more normal operations. *Figs. 7* and *8* show various aspects of ripsawing, which is the cutting of a piece of wood right through along its length. For this work the riving knife should always be in place, its purpose being to keep the saw kerf open behind the blade. If it were not used, or if it were thinner than the blade in use,

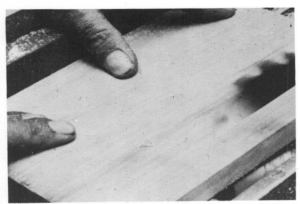

Fig. 7   Ripping edge
off wide board on
Wolf sawtable, with
blade tilted

Fig. 8   Straight ripping cut against
fence. Cut has been made from one
end, work reversed to complete

the wood might close up and pinch the back of the saw. Incidentally, where saws are used without a riving knife and guard, it is usually the back of the blade which causes the accidents when the saw kicks the wood back at the operator, dragging his hand with it.

Ripping is carried out by setting the rip fence at the required distance from the blade, allowing for the thickness of the blade plus its set, and passing the wood through, keep-

ing it in contact with the fence. Naturally a prerequisite is that the wood has a straight edge, and if it has not a line must be drawn, and the work ripped freehand to it. When ripping, the hand which is near the fence should always have one or more fingers hooked over it to give it an anchor. By the same token, the hand which is behind the sawblade should have some fingers hooked under the edge of the table if possible. I do not wish to appear pessimistic, and accidents with circular saws are not as common as some people think, but when they do happen they do so very fast and often the man who has been injured cannot remember what happened, so it is as well to be cautious.

Where long work has to be ripped it is often safer and easier to push the wood partway through, then go round to the back of the table and finish the cut by pulling on the wood. A little practice is needed, but once the knack has been acquired this is easy to do, and it saves wear and tear on the nerves! In ripping, the saw should project through the wood by

Fig. 9 Wolf Sapphire
drill and saw attach-
ment set up in a Wolf
sawtable. Note the rip
fence and mitre guide

not more than the depth of a gullet, or so the saying goes. In fact, if too much projection is given there will be a rougher cut.

Another way to deal with long work, which I always use at exhibitions, is to saw about halfway through, withdraw the wood, turn it end for end, and finish the cut. This gives complete control but it is not effective unless both edges of the wood are parallel.

Crosscutting is a word which covers a multitude of sins. Straightforward crosscutting is easy enough but there is quite a lot which needs to be said about other operations which come under this heading. Basically, in crosscutting, we are cutting through a piece of timber across the grain, but there is more to it than that and there are traps for the unwary. In crosscutting the mitre gauge is used, and it is a good idea to fix an auxiliary wooden fence to it. This should be tall enough for the saw to be taken right through it without severing it, so that measuring can be done from the saw kerf.

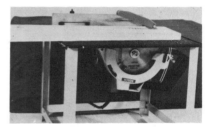

Fig. 10 Bosch portable saw fitted into small sawtable. This is a useful unit around the house

If you want a posh job you can let a piece of a wooden rule into the bottom front edge of the fence so that cutting off pieces of given length will be easy. If a number of pieces of the same length is required, a small stop block can be clamped to the fence at the appropriate point, and all that is required is to keep pushing the wood up to this and sawing through. It is advisable to have a rebate at the bottom of the stop block so that sawdust does not accumulate and affect the length of the cut-off.

Naturally, before any work of this sort is undertaken, the mitre gauge must be tested for squareness with the blade, using a square against the sawblade. A common error is the use of the rip fence as a length stop when crosscutting. Some people get away with this for quite a time, but it usually catches up with them in the end. If you want to use the rip fence for this, a block should be clamped to it, and used as a starting point. There will then be clearance and no fear of the severed piece twisting and jamming between the blade and the fence. This can happen and when it does the offcut can be thrown back with a great deal of force. Sometimes when a wide board has to be cut there is not enough room to get the mitre fence on to the table. If this should happen, the answer is to put the gauge behind the work and push it with the wood until it reaches the back of the table, when the cut can be stopped and the gauge brought round to the front to finish. Another good idea is to have a slot along the wooden fence on the mitre gauge, right through it, so that a small block can be attached by means of a bolt and a wing nut. This can be moved to any desired distance from the saw without any bother, and greatly facilitates crosscutting.

Many woodworking joints can be cut quickly and accurately on the sawbench, but the results will be better if the wood is run through a thicknesser first. The point is that for most of the joints, like half laps and T bridles, the wood is flat on the table and the blade is set to remove exactly half the thickness by means of a series of crosscuts. The setting of the blade is obviously very critical indeed for

work of this nature. If it is set too high or too low the joint will not fit flush.

The commonly accepted way to ensure accuracy in this is to take a piece of scrap from the material to be used and set the blade projection so that when a cut is made from each side, *Fig. 11*, just a few splinters of wood are left in the middle. It is essentially a trial and error affair, but it does not take long to get things right. Obviously, in this sort of work, the guard cannot be used, so due care must be taken. *Figs. 12* and *13* show some joints which can be cut, and in fact, the rather rough surface left by the saw is ideal as a key for the adhesive.

Tenons can be cut by this method too. Scrap material is again used to get the setting correct, and there is no need to cut a whole tenon to try the fit as just one saw cut across each side of the wood at the extreme end will do, adjusting the set of the saw projection until the fit is as required. Should it be necessary to haunch the tenon, it can be done in a similar manner.

The cutting of mitres for picture framing and so on always seems to present problems to the beginner, but it can be done easily enough on the home sawbench in a number of ways. Some of these involve the use of home made jigs, which I will deal with later, but for the moment, let us consider the cutting of mitres with the mitre gauge itself. It should, of course, be a simple matter yet in fact it is anything but!

In the first place I have yet to see a really good mitre fence which is

Fig. 11 Cuts made from opposite faces to check setting in tenoning. The saw requires a fraction more projection

easily read and easily set with accuracy, except on one or two large and very expensive sawbenches. The usual cheap and nasty affairs require the eyesight of an eagle plus a great deal of luck to achieve an exact setting, and anyway the markings are so thick that one can be half a degree out with no trouble. I am unable to understand why no-one has invented a mitre fence which can be set to the vital forty-five degree position easily, but there it is. The answer is to make a template from plywood or hardboard, which is exact, and to set the gauge from this. Having done so, the mitres can be cut in either the open or the closed position, *Fig. 14*, and this is a matter of personal preference, though I always like to work with my fingers as far as possible from the blade.

Cutting mitres in this manner will introduce the beginner to a phenomenon known as creep, which can be a real nuisance. What happens is that the action of the saw tends to make the wood move slightly along the mitre fence during the cut, which obviously means that the cut will not be true and we shall have a badly fitting joint. There are several ways in which this can be reduced, if not entirely avoided. Firstly, if the wood is held really firmly to the fence or better still clamped to it, and the cut

Fig. 12 A T-bridle joint cut on the sawbench

Fig. 13 Part of a half-lap joint being cut over the sawblade

Fig. 14 Showing mitre gauge in open and closed positions

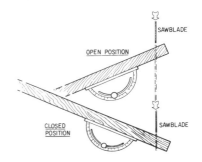

made slowly, creep will be almost non-existent. Secondly, one can attach a strip of coarse abrasive paper to the front of the mitre fence, or a number of small pointed brads can be set into the wooden sub-fence with just their tips showing. Either of these procedures will virtually eliminate the problem if the wood is held sufficiently hard against the fence.

Rebating, wherever possible, is done on the planer, which deals with it in one operation. Sometimes it may be necessary to use the saw for rebating, and the method is as follows. The wood is marked out, and the saw is set to take the cut into the edge first, which will mean that when the second cut is taken the work will be flat on the table and receiving maximum support. The first cut into the edge is not taken to the full depth but

a little less; when the second cut is made with the saw set to the full depth, it will leave a clean corner.

It is never a good idea to stand directly behind work on a circular saw if it can be avoided. This applies particularly when rebating, as the section of wood which is cut out is often ejected at high speed towards you. This is not likely to hurt very much, but it can startle you, and being startled while using a sawbench is not good. This problem does not occur if the cuts are made in the reverse order with the section being cut out facing away from the fence, but there is little support left with the work on edge like this, and if you have a wide gap round the sawblade it is possible for the corner of the work to drop down into it.

The sawbench is used a good deal for

Fig. 15 Partly assembled pusher block for use in cutting or grooving small pieces

Fig. 16 Adjustable tapering jig for sawbench. It can be opened to give the required cut and locked by means of a screw

Fig. 17 Tapering operation. Jig and work move together

grooving operations of various kinds, and a block should be made up as shown in *Fig. 15*. It will be seen that this enables the work to be pushed forward and downward at the same time, and it is also a useful item when small pieces of wood have to be cut. Tapering is an operation often performed on the sawbench, and although it can be done in a freehand manner by sawing to a marked line, decidedly better results will be obtained by the use of a jig, especially in repetition work, *Figs. 16* and *17*. If you anticipate doing much of this sort of work it is worth making one of the adjustable variety. It will not take very long to construct and will be found most useful. Its size is not critical, except that it must be made high enough for the slotted piece to clear the top of the fence. What is needed is some wood say three inches by half an inch. Take two pieces of this with a length roughly the same as that of the sawtable and hinge them together as shown, letting the hinges in so that they can be closed right up. As the photographs show, there is a stop block at the back end on one leg of the jig and also a slotted piece of wood or metal across the top, which connects the two so that they can be clamped in any selected position by means of a wing nut. This jig is designed to ride against the fence as shown in the illustration, being slid along the fence and pushing the wood into the sawblade by means of the stop block.

To make, say, some legs for a stool, it is first necessary to work out either the taper required per foot, or the taper overall. If you are working to a

taper per foot of $\frac{1}{4}$ in., all you need to do is to measure exactly 12 in. back from the centre of the hinge and open the jig by $\frac{1}{4}$ in. at this point. The work is now placed in position on the jig, and two adjacent sides are tapered. Now it becomes necessary to open the jig by a further $\frac{1}{4}$ in., because if one of the sides which have already been tapered is placed against the jig, the two angles will cancel out and the wood will be parallel to the blade. Should you be working to a taper of $\frac{3}{8}$ in. in 15 in., the taper would simply

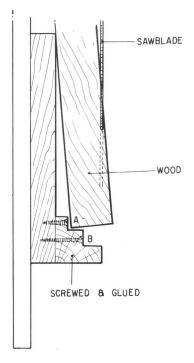

Fig. 18   Non-adjustable tapering jig for repetition work

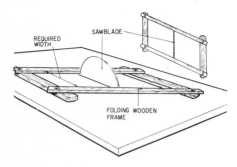

Fig. 19 Folding frame establishes position of batten for coving

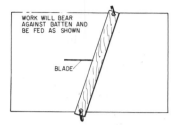

Fig. 20 Batten clamped to table acts as guide for work

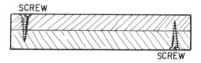

Fig. 21 Wood prepared for turning prior to coving

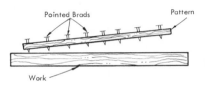

Fig. 24 Use of brads in pattern when making table mats

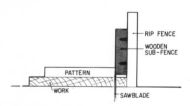

Fig. 22 Pattern sawing technique seen from front of table

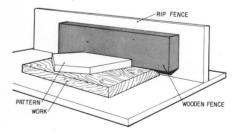

Fig. 23 This is an ideal arrangement for repetition cutting of straight sided shapes

be a matter of opening the jig by $\frac{3}{8}$ in. at a point 15 in. from the centre of the hinge, and so on. A jig can be made as in *Fig. 18*, and this type is normally used where a certain special type of leg is in steady production. A guide board is made to ride along the fence, having at its end a piece of wood with two notches cut in it as shown. One of these notches gives the taper required and is used for the first two sides, the other notch gives twice the taper, and so is used for the remaining sides.

An interesting aspect of work on the sawbench is hollowing out lengths of timber, or "coving", as the process is called. I have done a lot of this at exhibitions and it always causes interest. Its practical uses are somewhat limited, but it is one of those odd operations for which there is a call from time to time, and so it is as well to know the mechanics of the matter. The basic idea is very simple indeed, and consists of having a batten or guide board fixed at an angle across the table and running the material against this over the saw-blade. This is given an initial projection from the table of $\frac{1}{8}$ in., increasing by this amount with each successive pass of the wood.

The setting up for cove cutting is quite easy. It is first necessary to make a folding frame as shown in *Fig.* 19, and having set the blade projection to the full depth desired for the cove (say 2 in.) the folding frame is adjusted so that it just touches the back and front edges of the blade. A pencil line drawn along the inside of the frame as in *Fig. 20* will now give the setting position for the guide batten, which must be clamped firmly to the table. All that now remains is to reduce the depth of cut to $\frac{1}{8}$ in., make the first pass steadily and continue, increasing the depth each time until the full depth is reached.

This operation has its values for the woodturner, too. Two pieces of wood can be clamped together as in *Fig. 21* and turned to a true cylinder. Usually a piece is left square at each end to take a screw or two just to be safe, although the pieces of wood are glued together with paper in between. These are split apart after turning, and coved. They can now be cut to lengths, have bottoms fitted to them,

and be turned into vases, tankards, tobacco humidors, and so on.

The point here is that a good deal of rather laborious and awkward turning can be avoided. Coved work like this will not be truly round inside, but this does not matter a great deal as it can soon be made so on the lathe.

One very useful method of sawing is often completely overlooked, which is a pity, because it can save so much time. I am referring to what is known as "pattern sawing". It is the same idea as is used by the turner to dress back overhangs on laminations when building up post-blocked blanks for table lamps and the like. *Figs. 22* and *23* illustrate the idea clearly, and the arrangement does not take long to set up. You screw a wooden fence to the rip fence, leaving a gap between it and the table just sufficient to allow the work to slide under, and the sawblade is set in exactly flush with the edge of the wooden fence. If, for example, you wished to make a number of octagonal table mats, a pattern would be made and a few small sharp brads allowed to protrude from its surface, *Fig. 24*. Squares of material for the mats can now be temporarily attached to the pattern by means of the brads, and the edges of the pattern run along the fence to cut off the corners. All the mats will be identical and there is no danger involved in the cutting. Other applications of this principle will no doubt occur to you.

CHAPTER 6

Sawbench accessories and attachments

THERE are quite a number of accessories and attachments for use with sawbenches which we will deal with in this chapter, but before we start on that, let us give just a little attention to the matter of running up mouldings on a sawtable. Quite how many it is possible to make I cannot say—the limit is the ingenuity of the individual, but some very attractive ones can be produced.

A common moulding used for decoration on furniture is shown in *Fig. 1*, and can be made quite simply, many feet run being produced from a single piece of wood. A wooden fence is attached to the mitre fence and a pin, in fact a nail which has been driven in and the head nipped off, is positioned according to the shape of moulding required. The mitre gauge is set square to the blade, and the saw allowed to project from the table by an amount equal to two-thirds the thickness of the wood.

The next operation is to prepare the board for cutting into mouldings, by crosscutting it repeatedly on alternate sides, using the pin as a spacing guide. When this has been done, the prepared material must be ripped into thin slices before it can be used. Ripping on work as thin and fragile as this is not easy unless a special set-up is employed, and I find it best to remove the insert from the sawtable, and replace it with a piece of hardboard or ply. If the table is lowered on to the blade while it is running a very narrow slot will be made, which will give complete support to the mouldings. The ripping should be done with a fine toothed sawblade, and preferably one which has recently been sharpened.

Fig. 1 When the board has been cut as described, the moulding is ripped off in thin strips

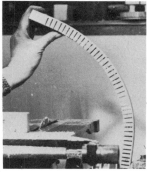
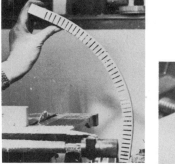

Fig. 3   Moulding block for sawbench. Cutters are firmly gripped by wedge action

Fig. 2   Wood which has been kerfed on the sawbench can easily be bent to shape and glued in position

Moulding like this can either be applied direct to the work, or mounted on strips of contrasting wood. In fact it looks well if it is let into such a strip, so that it comes flush.

Other types of moulding can easily be thought of, for instance one could cut grooves on one side of the wood only, perhaps wider than the saw itself, thus making a castellated effect when the wood is ripped.

Another use of this guide pin system is shown in *Fig. 2*, where cuts are being made from one side of a length of wood, through to about $\frac{1}{16}$ in. from the surface, at regular intervals. This is known as kerfing, and can also be done on a bandsaw. It is used to form a bend in a piece of timber. When the kerfing has been completed, the surface of the wood is wetted, the grooves are filled with glue, and the wood bent round and left under slight pressure until the

glue has set. When sanded off it will be very difficult to see how the bend has been made.

Now, what about accessories, jigs, and the like? Well, there are a number of these, but the two main accessories are the moulding block with its cutters, and the wobble, or drunken, saw.

Taking the moulding block first, this is an extremely useful device and is not used enough by the amateur, who tends to be afraid of it. Naturally, it can be dangerous if used foolishly, but with proper care and attention it is a real boon to the woodworker. It is felt by many newcomers to power work that the knives may fly out while the machine is running. This is very unlikely, and if in fact they were fitted properly in the first place, they will not do so. What can happen is that someone decides to be clever and take a full depth cut with a large cutter. On softwood one may get away with this but it is not advisable, and certainly not with hardwoods, which can cause the knives to snap off.

The parts of the moulding equipment are shown in *Fig. 3* with a selection of cutters. These can be bought in a large number of shapes, and also as blanks for filing or grinding to shape for special jobs. The moulding block itself is heavy, and well balanced, and on the type shown the cutters are held in place by wedges which are pulled down tight with Allen screws. The theory of using these things is that the two knives should run in exactly the same plane but this is not easy to achieve. If the knives are sharp and the feed rate kept fairly slow, the results will be quite good, even if only one of the knives is doing the cutting. The other acts as a balance, and helps to clear out the rubbish.

Ideally, as I have said, the two knives should be set exactly the same, but this is quite a problem. My own way of setting up a moulding block is no doubt rather primitive but it works, and so I stick to it. The sawtable is, or should be, a dead flat machined surface, so I loosen off the wedges in the block, clean out the inside (particularly where the cutters will seat) and lay the block on the table. Firstly we want to get the cutters true laterally, which is fairly easy. If small knives are to be used which are narrower than the cutter block, they can simply be fitted in so that they are lying on the table

surface and contacting the bottom of the slot in the block, then tightened securely. If larger knives are used, however, you can place washers or coins under the cutter block to allow the desired lateral projection of the cutter, *Fig. 4*, and proceed as before. In order to fit the moulding block it will obviously be necessary to remove the sawblade, and the table insert must be removed, and replaced with the special one provided. The block is now bolted into place, and the set-up is checked by hand to see that there is no chance of the cutters fouling anything when the machine is started.

Whenever a moulding block is used, a fairly thick wooden fence should be fixed to the rip fence, *Fig. 5*. The next move is to lift the fence well clear of the table, start the machine on its highest speed, and lower the fence slowly so that the cutter will make its own little arch in the wood. This arrangement has two purposes, in that it effectively removes any chance of the cutters striking the metal rip fence, and also allows the cutter to be partially covered by the wooden sub-fence, so that the shape it produces can be varied.

When I have reached this stage, I take a piece of wood and run it along the sub-fence into the cutters for a short distance. I then shut off the motor without moving the wood and inspect the situation from the rear, turning the block by hand to see whether, by any strange chance, both knives are contacting the work. If they are, I am agreeably surprised, and can go ahead with the job. If, as is more likely to be the case, one knife is low, I will adjust it as accurately as I can, check it again, and if all is well there is nothing more to worry about until the knives become blunt. Sharp cutters must always be used both for a good finish, and because blunt ones, like all blunt tools, are a source of danger. Blunt knives in a cutter block can easily kick the work back at the operator, who should not be standing in line with it anyway. I will explain how these are sharpened later—it is quite simple.

Work which is of reasonable dimensions can be fed to the cutters quite safely by hand, finishing with a push stick, but there are some problems which arise in connection with very thin or awkward shaped work.

It may be, for example, that the occasion arises for the running off of a number of very narrow mouldings, which could not be dealt with in the normal freehand manner without considerable risk. In cases like this, a piece of wood is attached to the rip fence, having a groove in its bottom face of a size which will accept the strips. These can then be pushed through, *Fig. 6,* quite safely.

Wooden springs can be used with

advantage for moulding work, both to hold the work down and to hold it in to the fence. Some manufacturers do in fact supply metal hold-down spring attachments, which are quite effective. When running a moulding right round a piece of work, such as a table top, the cuts across the ends should be made first, preferably with a piece of scrap to prevent too much spelching as the cutters break out. The cuts along the sides will then clean up any damage which has been done at the corners.

Fig. 7 shows a simple method of moulding the edge of circular work

Fig. 4   Method of setting cutter knives

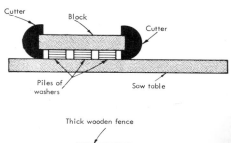

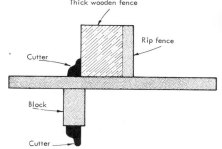

Fig. 5   A thick wooden fence is used, so that the cutters can be partly covered if desired

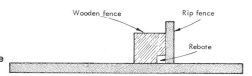

Fig. 6   Tunnel jig for moulding fragile strips

c

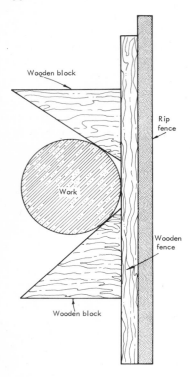

Fig. 7   Useful system for moulding circular work

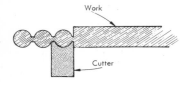

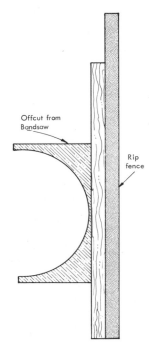

Fig. 8   Off cuts from bandsaw can be used in circular moulding

Fig. 9   Dowels can be made easily with a moulding block. Thin strips are left connecting the dowels, and are cleaned up afterwards

with the aid of two angled blocks, and in fact if the work has been cut out on a bandsaw, it is sometimes possible to use one of the offcuts as a guide, *Fig. 8*.

With the appropriate cutters and wood of the proper thickness, it is a straightforward matter to make your own dowels. If the thickness of the wood is correct, after a cut has been made from each side, there will be a sliver of wood connecting the dowel to the stock and this can be broken away and cleaned up with abrasive paper. *Fig. 9* shows the idea. One simply runs a cut along one edge of

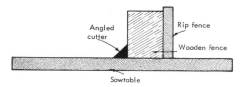

Fig. 10 Angled cutters used in stopped chamfering

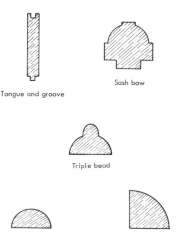

Tongue and groove

Sash bow

Triple bead

Half round

Quadrant

Fig. 11A Examples of mouldings made on a sawbench

the wood, then turns it over to make the second.

For some very fine work, the normal table insert provided may be too wide, allowing the work to drop into the cutters. In this case the insert can be removed and replaced with a hardboard or ply one, the knives being allowed to cut their own slot in this as the table is lowered with the motor running. This will provide full support around the cutters.

Other operations are possible with the moulding block such as the cutting of tenons and stopped chamfers. It may be that you have a planer on which the rear table is fixed, and if so you will not be able to use it for stopped chamfering. It can, however, be done quite easily with the moulding block and a pair of angled cutters, *Fig. 10*. It is as well to have the wooden fence long enough so that stop blocks can be used, to get the

chamfers the same all the way round. The operation is then the same as on a planer, placing the wood against the rear stop, lowering or rather swining it sideways into the cutters, feeding forward to the front stop, and lifting off. A very smooth finish will result.

The knives are kept sharp with a small file or coarse oilstone, leaving a burr on the face since it is this which does the work, as with the cabinet maker's scraper. Alternatively this burr can be removed, and the edge turned over with a piece of hard steel rod.

Some examples of mouldings made on the sawbench with block and cutters are given in *Figs. 11A* and *11B*. In order to make some of these

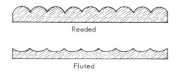

Reeded

Fluted

Fig. 11B Mouldings across grain. Thin slices can be ripped off and used as applied mouldings

mouldings there must be a method of spacing the cuts with absolute precision. This can be done in one of two ways, either by the guide board method, which has two separate ways of being used, or by using a board which is sacrificed in the process. In the former method, where a guide board is used, the idea is something similar to that used in the box-combed joint which we shall come to shortly. Whichever way the guide board is used it will be necessary to have a wooden fence attached to the mitre fence, with a spacing pin or strip let into it, *Fig. 12.*

In the first method a number of saw cuts is made across the board at set intervals according to the cutters to be used, the work is temporarily fixed to the guide board and cross cuts are made, using the spacing pin in the guide board slots. It is obvious, however, that this means that the cutters will cut into the guide board, and a better way is to have the guide board on top of the work, *Fig. 13,* though there is no backing here

to prevent the wood from spelching, which it will do because the cutting is across the grain.

Coving can be done with moulding cutter knives, and most efficiently too, but it is not possible to get as much depth as with the sawblade. The method used is the same as with the sawblade, a batten being clamped across the table at a suitable angle, and the work slid along it.

As we have already seen, the sawbench is a versatile piece of equipment, but it can be made even more so with a few simple home made jigs which will help us to do some of the more awkward jobs in safety.

If you want to do much mitring some sort of jig is really a must, because once you have made it and checked it thoroughly, it will cut a perfect angle every time. Two types are shown, *Figs. 14A* and *14B,* and both work very well, but the one in *Fig. 14A* is probably better. On sawbenches which have only one mitre groove, it is a good idea to make a runner which will slide along the side of the table, to make sure of the accuracy.

An easy way to make a mitring jig is to take a piece of plywood or blockboard and attach a strip of metal or hardwood to it which will fit the mitre gauge slot, *Fig. 15.* If

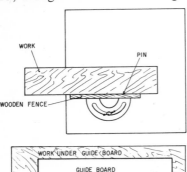

Fig. 12 Showing use of wooden fence with spacing pin

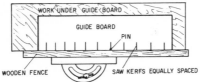

Fig. 13 Guide board on top of work, pin allows accurate spacing

Fig. 14A   Mitre jig for saw bench

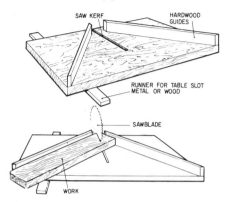

SAW KERF

HARDWOOD GUIDES

RUNNER FOR TABLE SLOT
METAL OR WOOD

SAWBLADE

WORK

Fig. 14B   With this cut, inside the guide boards, the work must be made the exact length before mitring

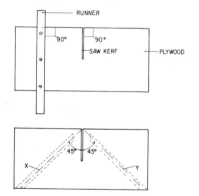

RUNNER

90°   90°

SAW KERF   PLYWOOD

45°   45°

X   Y

Fig. 15   Underside of mitre jig, top, showing runner parallel to saw kerf. Top face of jig, bottom, shows lines marked to set guides

Fig. 16   Mitring on outside of guides, work need not be cut to length first. Lower illustration shows another method, using 45-degree blocks

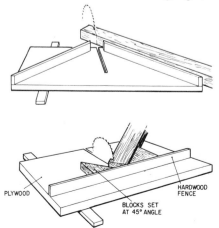

PLYWOOD

HARDWOOD FENCE

BLOCKS SET
AT 45° ANGLE

this is now placed in position on the sawtable and fed forward into the blade so that a cut is made about two-thirds of the distance across the board, all we have to do is to mark a line each side of this at exactly forty-five degrees to the cut, see the lines marked X and Y at the bottom of *Fig. 15*. This is done with a protractor and a hard pencil, and must be executed with extreme care. Hardwood guides can now be fixed in position along the guide lines, using glue and small screws. This jig will be as accurate as you have made it, so if it does not cut perfect mitres, don't blame me!

With a jig of this type, the wood will need to be cut exactly to length before the mitring is carried out. This is not necessary in the case of the jig shown in *Fig. 16*, however, as the wood being mitred is placed on the outside of the guide pieces. Another easy jig to construct is shown in *Fig. 16*, and needs only a straight piece of wood as an extra fence for the mitre gauge, with two forty-five degree blocks fixed to it. It is vital to see that the mitre gauge is dead square to the blade before using this.

The wobble, or drunken, saw is a useful part of the home worker's kit. It has numerous uses, such as rebating, grooving, and the making of the box combed joint, which with the adhesives available today is a very strong joint indeed. It is also neat and attractive and can be cut in a very short time. It tends to be used a lot these days in the construction of drawers and boxes, and in fact, with the machine set up ready and the timber cut to size, the cutting of the joints for a box or drawer can be done in three or four minutes with complete accuracy.

I feel that at this point I should explain, for those who are not familiar with this equipment, that there is a vast difference between a wobble saw as such, and wobble washers fitted and used with an ordinary sawblade. The former is the more expensive way of going about things, but it is a tool made and

designed for a certain function and it will perform well and accurately. The blade is a special stiff one, and the mechanism which regulates the amount of wobble is built into the saw. One of these is shown in *Fig. 17*. If wobble washers are used with a normal sawblade, however, one cannot really expect accuracy for the blade is too thin for the work and it is likely to whip in use.

Like any other sawblade, wobble saws must be kept really sharp if good work is to be done. On examination of the "works" of the wobble saw, *Fig. 18*, we find that there are numbers marked around it, which can be made to coincide with a register mark. It should be understood at the outset that these numbers do not mean anything in particular. I am often asked by woodworkers at exhibitions, and some who come to me for tuition, why these tools are not graduated in fractions of an inch or millimetres. There is a very good reason for this, and a little reflection will make it quite plain. A saw leaving

Fig. 17 Wobble saw has its own washers built in

Fig. 18 Centre part of wobble saw showing setting marks

the factory marked in such a manner would be most useful to its new owner, but only until such time as it became blunt enough for a visit to the saw doctor. On its return, its diameter would obviously be less and the markings would become progressively less accurate with each sharpening.

The real answer to this is to make up a guide board as soon as you get a wobble saw, *Fig. 19*, and make another every time the saw is sharpened. The saw is set on the machine, and a cut made into the edge of a piece of scrap wood, the resulting cut being numbered with a pencil. This process is repeated through the range of numbers, and if you want to be fussy about it the halfway positions can be done as well. This board will be a big help in determining what position the saw should be set to for any given job.

The wobble saw can be used for joint cutting if you wish since it can remove quite a lot of wood at one pass, and therefore speeds the job up. A point to remember, however, is that the bottom of a wobble saw cut is of necessity slightly radiused. For

most purposes in woodwork this is of no great moment, the radius being so slight, but it is as well to remember that it is there. This blade is excellent for such jobs as making strips of runner for sliding cupboard doors, or for tonguing and grooving.

Taking the construction of a simple box, or drawer, the first thing is to prepare the timber to be used. This must be perfectly square throughout, and preferably have been passed through a thicknesser. It may be that the box is square and therefore all the pieces of wood are the same length, or it may be rectangular. In either case, before any cutting is done, the four pieces of wood must be put into two distinct pairs and clearly marked so that there can be no confusion, because the two pairs are cut in different ways.

It is quite simple to make your own jig for box combing from a few scraps of material, but in the illustrations I am using the one supplied for use with *Coronet* machines. It is only the principle which matters, and a study of this will soon enable the handyman to make a jig for himself. Once the setting up has been done correctly one can cut joints all day with no bother, but it is vital to get these settings right in the first place. I normally make a joint from some scrap of the material to be used as a final check. The gauge, or jig, is fitted to the mitre fence, so it must first be established that the latter is dead square to the blade; it must be tightened so that there is no chance of it moving during the cutting. It will be noted that there is a wooden

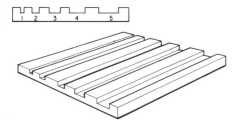

Fig. 19 Guide board for setting wobble saw, made from scrap

insert in this jig, secured by a wing nut. This is a spelch block, and its use is essential or the wood will be torn about where the wobble blade emerges. There are also two metal guides which are secured by screws, *Fig. 20* and can be adjusted.

Box-combed joints usually look best if the width of the cut is about the same as the thickness of the wood in use, so if we have timber $\frac{5}{16}$ in. thick, we will set the saw to give us a cut as close as possible to this. Having done so and tightened the saw securely with its nut, the next move is to set the correct projection of blade above the table. Theoretically this projection should equal the thickness of the wood, but in practice we lay a piece of the material against the sawblade, *Fig. 21*, and set the saw so that it projects just a fraction above the surface of it. This will mean that the pins of the joint will have a slight projection from the box when it is fitted together, thus enabling the joint to be sanded and

cleaned up without having to sand the whole box.

The next, and very important move, is to set the wobble saw by hand so that it has wobbled as far to the right as it will go. It is essential that the distance between an outward leaning tooth and the face of the nearer pin equals the width of cut, and this must be carefully measured. When the pin has been correctly set, the idea is that the other pin is set so that when a cut is made in the wood it will fit exactly over the two pins. Personally I never bother about this, simply keeping the work tight up against the first pin during the cutting, but this is a matter of preference.

The process of cutting the joint is another of those procedures which sound far more complicated than they really are, and a little practice will make an expert of anyone quite quickly. I have marked my pairs A and B, so I take one of the A pair, place it up against the pin, *Fig. 22*, and make a cut. The wood is now lifted off and the cut placed over the pins so that a second cut can be made, and we work our way across to the other side of the wood in this manner. Having done this the wood is turned end for end so that the same side is against the pin, and the process repeated. The second member of the A pair can now be treated

Fig. 21 Setting depth of cut— $\frac{1}{64}$ in. more than thickness of wood

Fig. 22 Cutting of first piece begins as shown

in the same way.

The cutting of the B pair is different. If it were not, the pins would meet instead of fitting together as a joint. Take the first of the A pair and place the first cut you made over the pins. It is a good idea to mark this first cut with a pencil when it is made. If the first of the B pair is now placed against the side of piece A, *Fig. 23*, a cut can be made which will be offset correctly. We can continue across the wood as before, laying aside the A piece. The

wood is now turned end for end and given exactly the same treatment, remembering that the offset must be given each time, and the last piece can be cut in a similar way.

If it is intended to use glue in the assembly of the unit, the joints should be cut to allow for their being slack enough not to squeeze out all the glue when they are put together. Some workers make them very tight so that they have to be knocked together with a mallet, and rely on one or two panel pins to hold them. The adjustment of the fit of the joint is done by moving the guide pin slightly to give a wider or narrower pin on the wood.

A good sanding will finish the job off, *Fig. 24*, and we have a very strong box. Some workers prefer to use a dado head for this job since this can be set to give a cut of known width and there is no radius in the bottom of the cut, but as I said earlier the radius is slight, and hardly discernible. Dado heads are very useful but they are not tools for the amateur to sharpen—unless you are an expert, it will pay you to take the dado to someone who is.

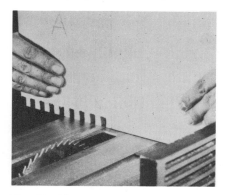

Fig. 23 First cut on "B" piece (right) is set up as here

Fig. 24 The finished joint. A good sanding will finish the job

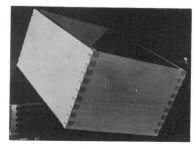

CHAPTER 7

Mortisers and mortising

THE mortice and tenon is still one of the strongest joints for frame construction and will no doubt continue to enjoy considerable popularity, even though the advent of synthetic resin adhesives has made dowelling an attractive alternative. Today, however, there seems to be less time for everything, and the making of these joints calls for machinery to give speed with accuracy on repetition work. Mortices which were once carefully and laboriously chopped out with mallet and chisel can now be produced in a very short time, and with precision. There are several ways of cutting them, so we take them one at a time.

Fig. 1 shows a mortice being cut on the support table of a universal machine, using a rotary slot miller bit held in a chuck on the mandrel. This freehand method may, at first glance, appear to be dangerous but in fact it is not, as long as the work is held firmly down to the table. The cutter is taken in to its full depth at each end of the mortice, and the wood left between the holes is then removed by cuts of roughly $\frac{1}{8}$ in., by sliding the wood across the fence. The depth can be controlled by a collar or "G" cramp on the bar of the table fence, *Fig. 2*.

A far better idea is to have the

Fig. 1   Cutting a mortice on combination table of universal machine

Fig. 2   A cramp on the fence bar of the table controls the depth

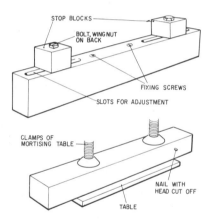

STOP BLOCKS

BOLT, WING NUT
ON BACK

FIXING SCREWS

SLOTS FOR ADJUSTMENT

CLAMPS OF
MORTISING TABLE

NAIL WITH
HEAD CUT OFF

TABLE

Figs. 4 and 5 Wooden fence for
mortiser, with adjustable stop blocks,
above. Below, jig for cutting circles in
ply using small slot miller bit. Small
hole is drilled in the work to fit it on
the nail. Wood is pivoted on nail or pin
of jig, fed into cutter, and revolved to
cut a circle

proper mortising attachment as designed for the machine, *Fig. 3*, which
has stops to limit the length and
depth of the mortice, and a control
to raise or lower the worktable to
centralise the cutter. The work is
clamped to the table and fed by
levers, one traversing the wood across
the cutter, and the other feeding it
forward. Once one of these attachments has been correctly set up,
large numbers of mortices can be
cut in a short time and there will be
no inaccuracy.

The slot miller bit is preferable to
the hollow square chisel for this type
of mortiser because there is less
strain on the machine, and no fuss
about the setting up. A wooden
fence should be fixed to the mortising
attachment, *Fig. 4*, to prevent damage
if the cutter breaks through the work.
It is then possible to set up stop
blocks on this wooden fence so that
the work can be pushed up to them,
clamped in place, and the mortising
done without the necessity for measuring or marking out.

The slot miller bit is a very fast
and free cutting tool, and if it is
looked after and not allowed to
knock against other tools in drawers
and boxes it will remain sharp for
long periods. These cutters can also
be used for grooving and slotting,
as their name indicates, and they
are very good for work of this nature.
By means of a jig similar to the one
shown in *Fig. 5*, it is possible to cut
out circles from plywood with them.

For those who do not possess a universal machine, tools such as the *Wolf* mortiser, *Fig. 6*, will do a good job. They will execute excellent work if properly set up, and this is not a long job when you have done it once or twice. I will explain the methods of setting up and using these machines, and I think the illustrations will help to clarify the operation. Two important points to watch when setting up mortisers of this type are that the edge of the chisel is dead square to the mortice, otherwise the cut will be rough, *Fig. 7*; that there is roughly $\frac{1}{32}$ in. clearance between the auger and the chisel at the end where the auger emerges. If more clearance than this is allowed, the chips will be too large and jam in the chisel, and if less is given the auger may rub the end of the chisel, and overheat (*Fig. 9*).

The operation of the machine is quite a simple matter. The base of the mortiser has a bar across it which can slide in slots, and is secured by wing nuts. This locates the wood. Attached to the column of the tool is a forked plate which can be adjusted just above the work and prevent it from being lifted up when the chisel is withdrawn. This plate carries two brackets which can also be secured by wing nuts, and these are adjusted so that they just touch the work at the back so holding it in position. The tool is set up so that the wood can slide freely between the clamps but cannot move either forward or back. If the mortice is to go right through the wood there must be some scrap wood used as packing under the job, to prevent damage to the

cutter and spelching of the wood. On the column of the mortiser there is a depth stop which can be set as required.

These machines are very good indeed, and will give long service if they are looked after as they should be. The mortice is marked out and the wood lined up for the first cut, *Fig. 8*. This first cut is a heavy one because the whole of the cutting edge of the chisel is used. The drill goes in, breaking up the wood, followed by the chisel itself. This must always be kept sharp, and will trim the edges to give a square cut.

The first cut, as I said, is a heavy one, so it should be taken in stages rather than in one movement, withdrawing the cutter once or twice to clear the chips. The remaining cuts which complete the mortice are taken using only about two-thirds of the chisel each time, so they are far easier and can go to the full depth in one movement. A little practice with one of these mortisers will soon show how simple the job really is, and how quick and efficient. When correctly set up they can be used for cutting tenons and half laps, but scrap wood should be used as packing to prevent the chisel from bending away from the work, *Fig. 8*.

In *Fig. 10* you can see the special tool by which the hollow square chisel is sharpened, using a hand brace or a hand drill, but the outside edges must never be touched. Since these machines are, in essence, drill presses, they can in fact be used as such, and in *Fig. 11* you can see the small device which is supplied to change the tool over for

Fig. 6   Wolf mortiser

Fig. 7   The chisel must be square to the work

Fig. 8   Wolf mortiser cutting first side of a tenon. Note packing to support chisel

Fig. 9   Business end of chisel mortise cutter

Fig. 10   Cutter for sharpening the chisels

Fig. 11   With the
attachment shown, the
mortiser can be
adapted to become a
drill stand

drilling. Items as small as this are
always difficult to find when they
are wanted in a hurry (or so I have
found) so it is as well to label them
and keep them in a safe place. *Fig. 9*
shows a close-up photograph of the
business end of an auger for a chisel
mortiser, and you will note that it is
not quite the same as a normal Jen-
nings pattern bit, in that it has no
point. Mortising with the hollow
square chisel can also be done very
well in machines such as the *Myford
ML8* woodworker, with the arpro-
priate attachments. The whole thing
is basically the same, except that it is
performed in a horizontal rather than
a vertical position.

A type of mortiser with which the
home woodworker is unlikely to
come into contact is the chain
mortiser. This is a large machine
used on big work, in factories and
is, in fact, very similar to a chain saw,
which is fed end-on into the wood.

CHAPTER 8

Sanders and sanding

ARLIER in the book we had a brief look at sanders as applied to electric drills, but there are some very interesting types of abrasive machinery available at reasonable cost—reasonable, that is, to the man who has the use for it, and will recover his capital outlay.

Firstly, let us consider the disc sander. I am not talking now about the rubber-backed device for the electric drill, but a robust accurate tool which can be used for a wide variety of purposes. These are extremely useful tools, but it is as well to remember that the life of the discs is governed by the amount of use they get and the type of material on which they are used, so they should not really be employed to take off large quantities of wood which could have been trimmed with a saw.

Abrasive discs are easily obtainable from good tool stores, but if you have a machine such as the *Myford ML8* or the *Coronet*, you will be well advised to buy the type recommended by the maker of the machine. He is anxious for you to get the best from it, and has carried out research to establish the best papers for the tool.

As far as the machines mentioned are concerned, the disc sander is one of the attachments. It may have a fixed table which can be brought up close to the disc, or it may have a specially made tilting table to enable angled sanding to be carried out. On universal machines the sanding disc is usually made of alloy of some kind, and is fitted to the mandrel of the lathe, *Fig. 1*. Special adhesives can be purchased for sticking the

Fig. 1 Sanding plate being fitted to lathe mandrel

paper to the disc, and these should be used wherever possible. If you should run out, *Dunlop* rubber solution such as we mended our bicycle tyres with in far off days will do very well, but never use glue. The adhesive should be applied to both surfaces, allowed to dry, and then the paper stuck on. If any difficulty is experienced in removing it when it is worn out, a little warming will help. Personally, unless the discs are torn, I apply them one over another until there are about four on the plate, and I find that they then come off fairly easily.

The sanding table should be kept close to the disc so that there is no danger of anything being dragged down between the two, and it should be just a fraction below the centre line. When using the sander, only the side which is going downwards is used, *Fig. 2*, since this helps to hold the work down on the table and the majority of the dust and rubbish is

carried away from the operator—who should be wearing a mask.

For two reasons, the pressure of the material against the sander should be light. One is that it will remove wood very fast, and the other that if too much pressure is applied the wood may be burnt by friction. Wherever possible, keep the work moving from side to side on the disc, as you would move sandpaper from side to side when sanding turned work in a lathe. This allows the dust to get away, and prevents build up of heat at one spot, together with loading of the abrasive paper. When straight pieces of wood are being sanded along their edges only very light pressure can be applied as too much will cause ridges to appear.

This type of sander is not intended for finishing work, since the path of the abrasive granules crosses the grain, but it is a good tool for cleaning up and for general shaping and rounding of corners. Unless angle

Fig. 2 "Downstream" side of disc is used, so that work is not lifted from the table

Fig. 3 Sanding radius to pencilled line

sanding is to be carried out, it is as well to check with a square to ensure that the disc and the table are at ninety degrees, otherwise work may be spoiled.

One of the most useful applications of this tool is shown in *Fig. 3*, where radii have been marked on a straight workpiece and are being trimmed. With some practice this can be done perfectly, though a good deal of wear on the disc can be avoided by cutting some of the waste away on a saw first. Rough circles, which have been cut out for toy wheels or similar purposes, can be sanded true by means of a simple jig as shown in *Fig. 4*. The circles are pushed on to a pointed brad in the blockboard jig, fed forward until the disc just cuts, and the jig is clamped with a "G" cramp to the table. The workpiece is then steadily rotated until it is completely round.

The finishing of the ends of mitres which have come from the saw can be carried out with the disc sander by fixing a batten on the table at the correct angle, and feeding them lightly up to the sander. Naturally the setting of the batten is very critical, and it is as well to sand one piece and check it carefully before proceeding, *Fig. 5*.

Discs of this nature do become loaded with wood particles after a time, but this can be alleviated to some degree by pressing a piece of plastic hosepipe or hard rubber against the upward moving side of the disc. The abrasive will wear away some of the plastic, but a lot of the wood will be cleared out, and the life of the disc can be prolonged considerably in

this way. The downward moving side of the disc should not be touched in this procedure, just in case of accidents due to jamming between plate and table. A lot of talk goes on about making tilting sanding tables for use with this sort of sander, but I

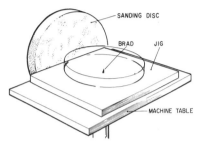

Fig. 4   A simple jig for sanding circles

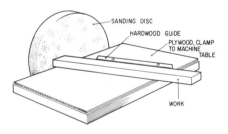

Fig. 5   Jig for angle sanding

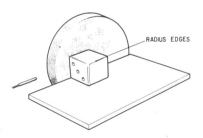

Fig. 6   Sanding wooden dice for cigarette lighter mounts

have never found this to be necessary. I normally use a bevelled strip cut at a suitable angle to the table, and feed the stock over this. If the angle is marked upon it, and the strip kept, it can be used repeatedly. ·

A disc sander which has been accurately set to ninety degrees can be used for trimming blocks, as in the making of the dice shown in *Fig. 6*. There are two other types of sanding machines, which concern us, namely the belt sander and the orbital sander.

I am aware that belt and orbital sanding attachments for drills can be obtained, but what I am now referring to is the industrial type of sander, which is beautifully made and capable of sustained periods of hard and accurate work. I use both, and would be lost without them.

A belt sander, *Figs. 7* to *9*, has an endless belt like the track of a tank running over two drums, with provision for tracking it so that it will run centrally. These belts can be removed and changed in a moment, simply by moving a lever to release the tension. The good ones have a dust extraction unit, with a bag rather like a domestic vacuum cleaner, and if you want to see just how much stock they do move, try running one without its bag!

As with other sanders, various grades of abrasive belting can be obtained, and a very good finish can be achieved with the tool because the abrasive grains run with the grain of the wood, or should do if the tool is used correctly. Belt sanders are used mainly on jobs with large areas but they are quite at home with smaller stuff if it is firmly clamped. Sanders of this type come in a variety of sizes up to really big ones weighing twenty five or so pounds, for use in joinery works and the like. A carbide insert is fitted in some of these tools, *Stanley* being one, to prevent the belt from cutting into the machine.

A belt sander takes a little getting used to. It is all very well to take one home from the shop and think that it is just a matter of moving it about on the work to get a first class job, but this is not, unfortunately, the case. It is largely a question of touch

Fig. 7 Powerful belt sander by Wolf Tools. Note tracking control knob at side

Fig. 8 Bosch belt sander unit designed to be powered by a drill

Fig. 9 Bosch industrial belt sander

good surface finish. I say a very good surface finish, because in fact there is nothing to touch the surface left by a good orbital sander.

Today's abrasive papers are streets ahead of those in use a few years ago, and there is a paper to suit every job. To get the best from an orbital sander it should be allowed to run under its own weight, which is quite sufficient, and it is important to see that the paper is stretched as tightly as possible over the carrying plate, or some of the orbital action will be lost. To produce a really first class finish on a piece of work, start with a medium grade of paper and go over the whole surface, lifting the tool from time to time to allow the dust to escape. Then change to a fine grade and repeat the process without hurrying, and finish by going over the whole thing again with an ultra-fine flour grade. This may sound like a lot of work, but if you do it that way you will have a perfectly finished surface. The *Wolf Sapphire* orbital sander has a speed of 14,000 rpm running free, which is very fast indeed, and it is an excellent tool. You may find it worthwhile to wet the surface of the work before the final sanding, and allow it to dry thoroughly. This will raise the grain, and the results will be excellent.

which comes with practice, and until you have acquired this you may find that there are distinct ripples and bumps in the surface of your work. Usually there is a trigger type switch in the handle of the tool, and between the two drums there is a flat pressure plate. These tools should be kept moving on the work, never stopping in one place, or marks will be made which may be hard to remove.

I normally hold the belt sander so that it is diagonal to the grain of the wood, moving it back and forth with the grain until I am satisfied that sufficient material has been removed. I finish off with a fine belt in order to get the smoothest possible surface, and with the sander in line with the grain.

The big belt sander is the real "strong man" of the sander family, being capable of removing large quantities of wood in a short time; with an open coated abrasive it will take paint off back to the wood in no time, and even so it can give a very

Fig. 10   Willow belt sander. I use one
of these a great deal

Fig. 11   Sanding
curved work on the
end of a Willow
sander. Makers are
Willow Tools Ltd.,
Molesey, Surrey

Another type of power sander is the
belt sander which is fixed, the work
being brought to it. Such tools as the
Willow Whippetoff are a good example of this, *Fig. 10*. These are very
useful for small pieces which would
be very difficult to deal with on a
hand-held belt sander, since this
might snatch them and injure the
fingers. The tools have a fence, which
is adjustable, and can be set at
ninety degrees or any other angle up
to forty five.

At one time I used to do a lot of
toy making and I found that one of
these was worth its weight in gold. As
a matter of fact, at least one manufacturer of universal machines offers
this tool as an attachment to his
product, and very well it performs
too. With the fence set at ninety
degrees, these tools are marvellous
for trimming the ends of stock dead

square, and their curved ends can
be useful for the sanding of curved
work, *Fig. 11*.

There is another type of sander in
common use, (mainly by wood-
turners) this being the bobbin sander.
It has a multitude of uses, according
to its shape, and some are shown in
Fig. 12. These are easily turned up on
a chuck in the lathe, and the work
is applied to them. Usually they do
not last long because they are small
and the paper wears out quickly, so
the turner makes them with a sawcut
down one side, *Fig. 13*. The ends of
the abrasive paper can be tucked in
and secured by driving a strip of
softwood in behind them. A radius
sometimes has to be sanded on to the

Fig. 12   Turning up a bobbin sander
for small work. Saw cut will be made
along pencil line to take ends of
abrasive paper

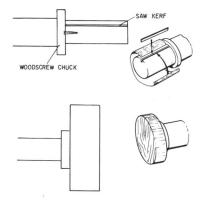

SAW KERF

WOODSCREW CHUCK

Fig. 13   Showing construction of bobbin sander

Fig. 14   Scrap wood turned to diameter of table pillar, to make bobbin sander for producing concave surface at ends of table legs where they join the pillar

leg of a table before it can be fitted to its circular central pillar, and here the principle of the bobbin sander comes into its own. A wooden bobbin is turned up with the exact diameter required for the inside of the end of the leg, *Fig. 14*, and the shape can quickly be made.

CHAPTER 9

The bandsaw

THIS is a tool for which I have the deepest sympathy! By the word bandsaw in this case I am referring to small tools, that is with throats up to about eighteen inches; the throat of a bandsaw being the distance between blade and column, *Fig. 1*. Anything bigger than this is rather out of place in an amateur workshop, but some very large machines indeed can be seen in joinery works. The small variety is, however, one of the most maligned tools I know of, and now I speak from bitter experience, having spent several years trying to explain to new owners of these tools that they just had not got the hang of the saw. There is a saying in the woodworking trade that some men can use a bandsaw while others cannot, and with this I must agree entirely, having met quite a few of the latter! Each time a blade breaks the saw is blamed, yet another man might well have got far more life out of it. It should always be remembered that the bandsaw is a tool for shape cutting. This is the purpose for which it was designed and it does it very well, but when it comes to cutting straight lines it is not by any means as good as the circular saw.

There are two types of bandsaw, the two-wheeled, and the three-wheeled. The advantage of the third wheel is that it is possible for a three-wheeled bandsaw to have a greater throat clearance. One rarely gets something for nothing in this world, however, and such advantage as is offered by the third wheel is to some extent offset by the fact that the wheels are smaller. Perhaps at first this may not seem to be a very serious

Fig. 1 Throat of a bandsaw is measured from blade to column. This 15 in. Willow is a first class tool

matter, but in fact the greatest
enemy of the bandsaw blade is metal
fatigue, caused largely by flexing
round the wheels. Up to a point,
therefore, a bandsaw with two wheels
will give a longer blade life than one
with three small ones. There are,
however, other factors affecting the
matter, and there seems little doubt
that the three-wheeler is the more
popular with amateurs today. The
owner of the three-wheeler need not
feel too despondent because when he
thinks about it, he will realise that
his blade is in contact with roughly
a third of each wheel rather than
approximately half, as is the case with
a two-wheeled machine. Controversy
will always rage over this, so I will
leave the reader to make his own
decision. Rather than skimp the job
of writing about bandsaws it would
be better not to write at all, so I will
do my best to cover what is, in fact, a
lengthy subject and a controversial
one, too.

There are, to my mind, two distinct
aspects to be covered here, the first
being the mechanics of the tool, its
adjustments, faults, and likely problems; the second, the actual use of
the tool and how to get the most from
it.

Let us take the mechanics first, for
if they are not right, the tool will
perform badly.

There is no need to stretch the
blade of a bandsaw like a violin
string, all it requires is sufficient
tension to permit the driving wheel

to do its job without slipping. The
idea that the tighter a blade is
stretched the better it will cut is a
fallacy.

There are certain requirements for
a good bandsaw which is to be a
friend and ally to the woodworker in
his shop rather than an eternal
nuisance, and these are as follow.
The frame of the machine should be
such that it will not twist and flex
when the machine is in use, for if it
does, all other adjustments will be
affected. There should be a good,
large, machined table which can be
relied upon to remain flat and true,
and at the outer end of the slot through
which the blades are fed in, there
should be a clamp to prevent any
movement at this point. A mitre
gauge slot should be provided, and
it will have its uses if you can get a
blade to run dead true, but we will
come back to that. A rip fence is,
with some models, an optional extra,
and I am not really surprised. The
saw was not invented for ripping
along the grain in straight lines,

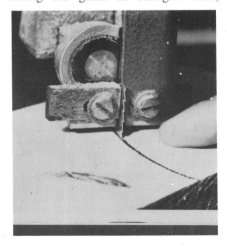

Fig. 2 Guides and thrust roller on Willow bandsaw

though it is worth a try if no better tool is available.

Bandsaws have thrust wheels to prevent the action of cutting the wood from pushing the blade back off the wheels, and small bronze guides to keep the blade from twisting—you can see what I mean in *Fig. 2*. This arrangement should be both above and below the table, and the table itself should have facilities for tilting to forty-five degrees. The guides come in a variety of materials, such as metal, wood, compressed fibre, and so on.

The front cover of the machine should be capable of quick removal for cleaning and adjustment, which

should never be undertaken unless the plug has been removed from the mains socket. *Fig. 3* shows the *Willow* 15 inch bandsaw with its front cover removed, and you will see the control right at the top which raises or lowers the upper wheel, thus increasing or decreasing the tension on the blade. When the machine has been in use and is to be left for a time, the tension should be relaxed a turn or

so, and re-applied when next the tool is used.

Bandsaw wheels have rubber tyres, which are normally vulcanised on. These tyres are "crowned", that is to say they have the sectional shape shown slightly exaggerated in *Fig. 4*. At the top rear of the bandsaw casing is the tracking control, which can be locked once it has been set. The purpose of this is to persuade the blade to run in the centre of the wheels, or for that matter, in any other position which may be considered desirable in view of the width of the blade in use. This control simply tilts the wheel on its axis, and it cannot be too strongly stressed that adjustments to

Fig. 3   The bandsaw without its front cover, showing internal layout

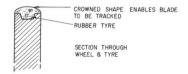

Fig. 4   Section of bandsaw wheel and tyre, showing curve of surface

it should never under any circumstances be made while the machine is running. The correct procedure will be described a little later.

When you receive your new bandsaw there will in all probability be a blade in it, and with luck you may find that this cuts quite well, and there are no problems. Do not allow yourself to be lulled into a false sense of security, however, for that blade will break sooner or later, and if you are not used to these tools it will probably be sooner! It is a fact that altering one adjustment on a bandsaw can put out others, and the tool has therefore to be set up in a definite sequence if good results are to be obtained.

The method given here is the one I use myself and as I have found it perfectly satisfactory it is worth a try, though there is no reason why you should not experiment if you wish. Let us assume that the blade in your machine has either broken or become so blunt as to be useless and that you therefore wish to change it. We will take the process step by step. At this point I would like to make it clear that if you follow this ritual you are unlikely to have much trouble with the saw, except for certain points which I will explain.

First of all, remove the plug from the mains, then take off the cover of the saw and put it out of the way. You will probably be surprised at the amount of sawdust which has collected inside the casing. Lower the upper wheel by means of the tension control and release the clamp at the front of the table slot, if any. The blade can now be taken out, broken into pieces, and put into the dustbin out of harm's way. At this point I normally bring on my trusty *Wolf* blower, which also doubles as a vacuum cleaner, and give the inside of the machine a good clean. The rubber tyres should be cleaned, and if you have cut much softwood you will find that they are encrusted with resinous deposits which will have to be scraped off. The guide blocks, both above and below the table should now be removed al-

together, and their ends examined for wear. If they are too badly worn they can be turned round so that the true ends go to the blade, or they can be filed true. The thrust wheels, which prevent the blade from being pushed back too far when cutting, should now be slacked off and moved as far backwards as they will go. It will be found with most small bandsaws that the blade guard is attached to the upper guide and roller unit, so this must be removed before the latter can be dismantled. Now, with a nice clean interior to the machine, we can put on a new blade, teeth pointing downwards! You may smile, but I have known them to be fitted the other way up, which is not at all difficult if the blade happens to be inside out. All the ironmongery in the way of rollers and guides should be well out of the way at this stage, so put the blade in place and tension it by means of the tension screw at the top.

The real problem for the new owner of a bandsaw is to know just how much tension to apply and unfortunately there is no real yardstick for this. It comes with experience, but my advice is not to overdo it. What we want is enough tension to drive the blade so that it does not slip under load, yet not so much that it is under heavy strain. Just for the moment tension it roughly, slightly under what you think it should have, and then turn your attention to the matter of tracking. Undo the lock nut on the track adjuster, and while turning the top wheel by hand in the direction in which it normally moves, alter the track by means of the adjuster until the blade is running about central. Now lock the tracking adjuster, and turn the wheel by hand again. It may be that the action of locking the adjuster has altered the setting slightly, so you will need to get this right before you can go any further. Never turn a bandsaw backwards, only in its normal direction of rotation. If you turn it backwards you will alter the tracking, and may even fetch the blade off the wheels.

Now the tension can be finally adjusted, and when you have it to your liking, you can turn your attention to replacing the thrust wheels and guides. The thrust wheels should be set to allow about $\frac{1}{16}$ in clearance between them and the back of the blade. It is most important that the blade is not allowed to rub them all the time. It should do so only when cutting or it will become case-hardened by frictional heat, and early failure of the blade will result. With these wheels correctly positioned and locked in place by their grub screws, the guides can be replaced.

An important point to remember is that the blade will move back by $\frac{1}{16}$ in. on to the thrust wheels when it is cutting, and allowance must be made for this otherwise the teeth of the blade may run between the bronze guides during the cutting, which will do no good to either. The setting of these guides should be such that they do not quite touch the blade, but nearly so—a state of affairs which can be brought about by placing a piece of paper between blade and guide on each side, then locking the guide and removing the paper. I must admit that I never bother, but that is the theory.

When all this has been done, both above the table and below, and the guides securely locked with the guard replaced, they must be adjusted fore and aft on their carriers. Do this so that when the saw is cutting the front of the guides will be just behind the gullets of the blade. This is important, and I advise you not only to get these settings correct when fitting a new blade, but to check them at regular intervals. If the teeth of a bandsaw are allowed to run between the guides, then the guides themselves will be damaged. This is serious, but there will also be damage to the sharpness and the set of the blade, which is far more serious, and will give rise to all sorts of problems.

DISC AFTER BAD BANDSAWING . SHOWING BOWED EDGE

Fig. 5   Bowed cut, due mainly to lack of set or blunt teeth

Do not try to correct the trouble shown in *Fig. 5*, where the blade is giving a bowed cut. This is due to lack or loss of set on the saw teeth, and the remedy is another blade. Remember to replace and tighten the table slot clamp, if fitted. The cover can now be replaced and secured firmly, and we are ready to use the saw. It is not a bad idea at this juncture to check to ensure that the table is at right angles to the blade.

Most machines have some sort of adjustable stop which enables the table to be reset correctly after having been tilted, but such things should still be checked sometimes.

There are multi-speed bandsaws, in fact the *Willow* illustrated here happens to be one, but single speed models are available, and a man who works only in wood will find one of these quite adequate for his needs as well as easier on his pocket. The tension of the driving belt must be kept correctly adjusted, and the machine oiled or greased in accordance with the manufacturer's instructions, and it should give you good service.

If you have any real problems, which is not likely, don't be afraid to contact the makers. They have a

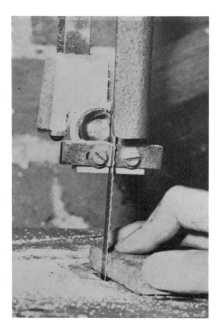

reputation to think of and you will find them helpful.

So much, then, for the mechanical part of the job, but how about the practical use of the tool? Let me say at once that small bandsaws often seem to have a will of their own and you are in for a few surprises once you begin to use one. One thing which must be borne in mind is that bandsaw blades are fine ribbons of steel, and at the time of writing, blade makers cannot guarantee exactly the same amount of set on both sides. The net result of this is that almost any bandsaw blade, new or otherwise, is likely to lead, either to one side or the other. If the amount of lead is slight, one automatically adjusts to it by feeding the work at a slight angle, but in bad cases the only answer is to hold a piece of emery wheel or coarse oilstone against the side of the blade which is leading, so dulling it. This is really a poor way of putting things right since we are blunting the blade to make it cut straight, but in extreme cases it may have to be done, *Fig. 6*. Do not overdo this or you will have the blade leading the other way, and by the time you have finished over-correcting there will be no teeth left!

Using the bandsaw ought to be a very simple matter indeed. Surely all one has to do is to push the wood into the blade and swing it about to follow the line? Up to a point this is true, but there is a great deal more to good bandsawing than may at first

Fig. 6   Abrasive stone being used to correct lead on bandsaw blade

appear, even on fairly simple jobs. There are also various jigs for use with the tool—quite a number in fact—and to get the best possible use from the machine one should know of them. They have been in use for years, "invented" time after time, and written about on many occasions, so I certainly claim no credit for them, but I will pass on some of the more useful ones.

As far as the power used to drive the machine is concerned, I would not recommend a motor of less than a half horsepower, and where heavy cutting is common a one horsepower would be better. There are some small machines like the *Burgess*, which have small motors and are eminently suitable for model making, toy making, and general light work.

The beginner may find himself confused by the rather large range of blades available but in fact, when he gets down to it, he will find that many of them are not applicable to his sort of work. Most of the time I use skip-tooth blades, either $\frac{1}{4}$ in. or $\frac{3}{8}$ in. wide, and for general use these are all I need. Standard blades have six or eight teeth, or rather points, to the inch and give a smooth edge, whereas a skip-tooth blade may have three or four. They cut faster, clearing the sawdust extremely well, but the edge left on the work is not so smooth. Most bandsaw cutting is done just outside the line and sanded back, so this does not matter unduly.

I receive numerous letters from woodworkers in all parts of the world seeking advice on various aspects of the craft and one which occurs very frequently is how one

should sharpen the bandsaw blade. The short answer to this is that with these little blades one does not bother, simply because by the time a blade has reached the stage where it requires to be sharpened, it will have passed round the wheels so many times that it will be badly fatigued and the large amount of time spent in sharpening the blade is likely to be wasted. If you want to touch up a blade which is fairly new but which has touched a nail or something similar, it can be fitted into the machine inside out so that the teeth point upwards. Each tooth is given one steady stroke with a fine file, straight across the face as in *Fig. 7*, and this will make a world of difference to it.

An alternative is to make up a jig as in *Fig. 8*, which will make the job easy. The thickness of the blade, as distinct from its width, has a great bearing on metal fatigue, and a lot to do with its life expectancy. It is usually said that a blade for this sort of saw should have one-thousandth of an inch thickness for each inch of wheel diameter, but this is not always strictly adhered to. The best bet is to use only the blades recommended by the maker. I also receive many enquiries about the possibility of repairing broken blades, and here again I doubt if it is worth the effort. They can be sent away for this treatment, but with the postage plus the repair charge and the fact that the blade may break as soon as it is used anyway the matter is, to say the least, debatable.

In practical sawing there are what amounts to a number of "tricks of

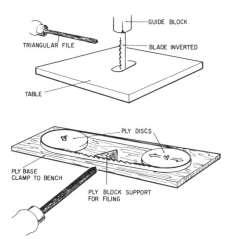

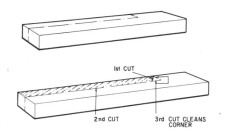

Fig. 8   Jig for sharpening bandsaw blades

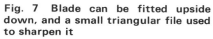

Fig. 7   Blade can be fitted upside down, and a small triangular file used to sharpen it

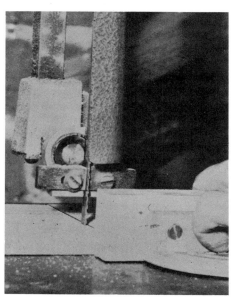

the trade" which should be learned at the outset to avoid unnecessary trouble. If they are not learned at the beginning they will certainly be found out the hard way later.

Having set up our machine we want to know how the blade is going to behave, and a quick way to find out is to set the mitre gauge exactly at zero and to make a cut across a board, *Fig. 9*. Any lead will be shown up immediately.

In *Figs. 10* to *13* I have shown various cuts which can cause trouble,

Fig. 9   Crosscutting with mitre fence set to zero, to check for blade lead

and indicated ways in which this can be overcome. Always study the job very carefully before you begin cutting, to save the embarrassment of getting the blade trapped. It is never advisable to back out of a cut,

Fig. 10   The shorter cut must be made first, or the blade may be pulled off the wheels when backing out. If work is too long for throat, first cut is made by swivelling wood against column, second cut removes shaded portion, final cut cleans corner

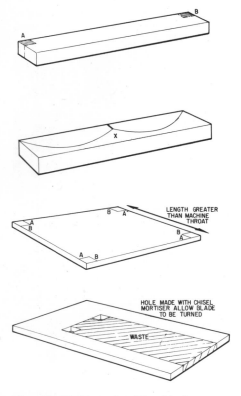

Fig. 11   Some work, when longer than throat, will need to be marked on both sides, cut A can be made, cut B must be marked on the opposite face of the wood. In lower sketch blade will be stuck at point X unless a short cut is made first as indicated.

Fig. 12   Another example of work which must be marked on both sides because of interference from column. Cuts A must be made with the surface shown upwards, the work is turned over to make cuts B.

Fig. 13   Holes cut with chisel mortiser will permit turning of blade

points to allow the blade to be turned, and I often use a chisel mortiser if the hole is needed in a square corner, *Fig. 13*. A wavy edged design, such as in *Fig. 14*, is best cut as indicated by following the outline roughly and doing the detail cutting later.

Blade width is important insofar as it affects the cutting of radii. If you attempt to cut too tight a radius with any blade the back of it will rub the work and become hot, leading to early blade failure. This is one factor that is directly responsible for the high rate of blade breakage which is suffered by beginners, who usually blame the manufacturer. If a cut has to be made which is obviously too tight for the blade, it is best to run in some radial cuts through the waste first, so that the small pieces fall

especially a long or curved one, unless this is really the only way for there is a fair chance of pulling the blade off the wheels. It can be done on short cuts, but even then, care must be taken.

Another point on which beginners often fall down is that there are occasions where the work must be marked out on both sides, or it will strike the column of the saw and it will not be possible to make the cut, *Fig. 11*. On intricate designs you will find it helpful to drill holes at strategic

Fig. 15 Radial cuts in to the line allow waste to fall away

Fig. 14 In a case like this most of the waste is cut away before the final shaping

away as they are severed so allowing the back of the blade to swing round, *Fig. 15.*

It will quickly be discovered that bandsaws cut better across the grain than they do with it, and we do not have rip and crosscut blades for them as we do for the circular saw. This is just one of those things to which you become accustomed and there is no real need to worry about it. A well known and useful idea with bandsaw work is known as pad sawing. It is just a matter of cutting several identical items at once in a stack, keeping them together by means of nails in the waste wood.

With all sawing, consideration must be given to the matter of safety. The bandsaw is a safer tool to use than the circular saw, but it will cut fingers and injure hands just as quickly if given the chance. Always work with the guard set just above the wood so that you can see the

Fig. 16 Always keep guard and guides close down to work

cutting line, but there is little chance of injury if your hand should slip, *Fig. 16.* Most injuries occur when the saw is near the edge of the wood—it suddenly breaks out and the sawyer's hand slips into the blade. This will not happen if the guard is set correctly, *Fig. 17.* Odd scraps and

Fig. 17 Ripping 3-inch sycamore. Note use of push stick, and correct height of guard

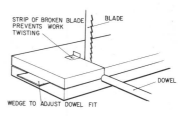

Fig. 19 Jig for ripping dowel stock for making mouldings

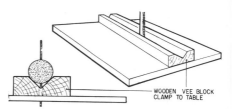

Fig. 20 Home made jig for ripping cylindrical stock

Fig. 18 Long board can be crosscut with minimum waste by pivoting against column, alternately from each side

bits of wood must be kept off the table, but do get into the habit of using a piece of wood for this and not your fingers. Many bandsaw accidents have happened through the nonchalant wiping of pieces from the table with the hand—it is quite possible to forget the blade.

Let us now examine the various operations for which we are likely to use the machine. There is, of course, straight ripping, sometimes

done on the bandsaw because of its narrow saw kerf. If there is slight lead on the blade it may be possible to adjust the rip fence to compensate for it, but if not, the rip fence can be removed altogether and a batten clamped across the table at an angle so that the saw will rip true.

Sometimes it may be necessary to cut through a board which is too long to be done by normal methods since it would strike the column. The answer here, provided the wood is not too wide, is to stand it on edge and cut it that way. An alternative method, involving a slight waste of timber, is shown in *Fig. 18*.

Most cutting on the bandsaw, whether ripping or crosscutting, is best done by marking the work clearly and sawing to the line rather than by relying on rip fences and mitre gauges. A useful jig to make for your bandsaw is shown in *Fig.* 19, and it is used for splitting dowel material to make half-round moulding. If you try doing this without a jig you will find that it is not as easy as it looks, but this little construction makes it quite easy. The cutting of cylindrical material, as for example in cutting turned stock in half lengthwise, is done as in *Fig. 20*, using a vee block which simplifies the process considerably.

Compound cutting on the bandsaw is best illustrated in the making of legs such as the cabriole or Queen Anne, *Fig. 21*. The wood for jobs of this nature must be prepared care-

be cut from the first side, the waste pieces being preserved so that they can subsequently be put back with nails or adhesive tape. This enables the markings to be followed and the work to receive support during the cutting. The leg itself, after cutting, will be finished off with hand shaping tools such as *Surforms*, preferably being held in the lathe for convenience. Compound bandsawing is used quite often in the preparation of blanks for carving and turning.

The matter of jigs for the bandsaw is an interesting one as the tool lends itself to this sort of thing. One of the most obvious is the jig for cutting circles and there are in fact two types, one for small diameter work, and one for large. For the cutting of small circles, a false table is made, as

Fig. 21 Compound bandsawing. A rough cabriole leg blank

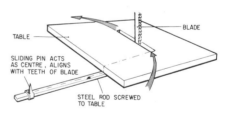

Fig. 22. Circle cutting jig. Clamp to bandsaw table.

fully, and it has to be square, not near enough. The work is marked out on two adjacent sides, as in the illustrations, using a plywood or hardboard template. Don't make the leg too fancy in design or you will have trouble in the cutting. A commonly used way of saving timber in this sort of job is to post-block the job as in turning by sticking pieces of wood on where required. When the work has been marked out it can

in the illustrations. It has a sliding strip in it with an anchor point, *Fig. 22*. For this sort of work a good blade should be used, that is, one which cuts as true as possible and does not tend to lead. A slight tendency to lead can usually be dealt with by shifting the position of the anchor point a little in relation to the blade. If only occasional circle cutting is required a very simple form of jig can be used, in the form of a board with an anchor pin, set in the correct position to give the diameter desired. More complicated jigs can be made if they are to have a lot of use, but the principle remains the same. Larger circles can be cut by means of an arm stretching out from the table with a movable point on it.

Kerfing, as done on the circular saw when wood has to be bent, can be done well on the bandsaw because the kerf is narrower and so permits more cuts to be made. This makes the job more flexible. The cuts are spaced about $\frac{1}{4}$ in. apart, and come to roughly $\frac{1}{16}$ in. from the surface of the wood, but this can be varied according to the bend in question. In order to save possible breakage the work is soaked with warm water.

The cutting of metal with a bandsaw does not concern us here, but with the right blades and speeds the tool is very good indeed for this job.

CHAPTER 10

The portable router

THIS is undoubtedly one of the most versatile and interesting of all woodworking tools, and at the same time, one of the least understood. There are many uses to which it can be put, in fact a claim frequently made is that the router is capable of performing ninety per cent of all woodworking jobs. It is not necessarily the best tool for all these operations, but with ingenuity there is very little one cannot do with it.

The principal feature of the tool and the one which gives it such versatility, is the extremely high rate of revolutions—the motor giving 27,000 rpm when running free, and still more than twenty thousand under load. Because of this it can cut both with and across the grain, leaving a surface of exceptional smoothness.

Before we look at the operation of this tool and what it can do we must consider its construction, *Figs. 1 to 4*. In its basic form the router is made up of two main parts, the motor, and the base. The series of photographs in this chapter will leave the reader in little doubt about the way the tool is made, but the precise setting of it is of paramount importance, and there are slight variations on the method among the makes. Apart from this, the basic principle remains the same. If the cutters are kept sharp this tool will give a smoother and cleaner cut than any other portable machine, and the more one works with a router, the more interesting it becomes.

We have seen that the essentials of the router are its motor and base. For the moment we will look at the *Stanley-Bridges* router. With this particular machine the on-off switch is recessed into the motor housing so that it cannot be knocked on accidentally, and a further refinement is fitted. With the plug removed from the mains, as it should always be when making adjustments or changing bits, the on–off switch can be lifted slightly when in the off position. If the chuck is turned a little by hand the switch will spring forward. The motor shaft is now automatically locked and only one spanner is needed to tighten or loosen the chuck. The motor housing has a coarse thread cut on it as the photographs show, four threads per inch in fact, and the adjusting ring is marked off in divisions of one sixty-fourth of an inch and further subdivided into quarters, so that a setting of a quarter of one sixty-fourth of an inch (0·004 in.) is easily made.

Until recently these tools were fitted with a light which illuminated the working area, but this has now been discontinued. The air intake for cooling is placed below the brush gear, so saving trouble with cleaning and servicing. The chuck, on the end of the motor shaft, is of the collet type, *Fig. 2*, and gives a very strong grip on the cutter shank. It should be

Fig. 1   Router motor casing, Stanley 267, showing coarse thread, and small stud which locates in base

tightened firmly but there is no need for excessive force. When inserting a cutter into the chuck always ensure that at least three-quarters of the shank goes in.

The base of the tool has two handles by which the machine is guided, and a wide opening so that the work can be seen easily. It is important to note that there is a small stud on the motor housing which engages with a particular slot on the inside of the base. Care must be taken to ensure that the two parts go together correctly and easily— never use force. The other slots are designed simply to reduce the surface contact and so to allow the motor to move freely in the base. On the bottom of the base, there is a black plastic sub-base designed to permit the tool to slide freely over the work surface without marring it. Also on the base of the router is a depth setting indicator, *Fig. 3*, and a lever clamp to hold the motor firmly when it has been set. There is no need to force this clamp lever as finger pressure will be sufficient.

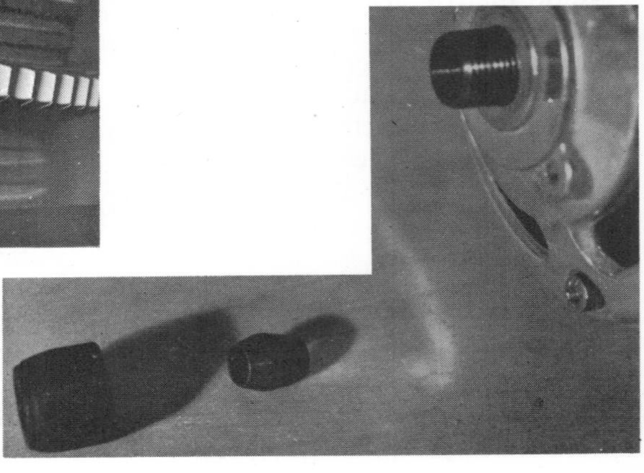

Fig. 2   Most routers have collet type chucks like this one

Assuming it is desired to make a setting of $\frac{1}{4}$ in. cutter depth, the procedure will be as follows. The router is placed on a flat surface in such a way that both base and cutter are resting upon it. The motor is clamped, the large adjusting ring wound up so that it is more than $\frac{1}{4}$ in. above the base, and the depth indicator pulled up so that its tab just touches the ring. Now the ring is wound down, pushing the indicator with it, until the latter shows the required setting. If the clamp is loosened and the router lifted from the bench, the motor will drop in the base by exactly the distance shown on the indicator, and the clamp can be retightened. When routing out recesses for hinges, or inlaying, a similar procedure is adopted but the depth indicator is not used. Instead, the hinge, or a piece of the inlay, is put between base and setting ring, so that it fits neatly without being punched, again with the base and cutter touching a flat surface. In this case when the clamp is released and the router lifted, the motor will drop by the exact thickness of the veneer or hinge.

A very important part of the equipment for a router is an attachment known as the straight and circular guide. This may sound somewhat paradoxical, but the fact is that the guide is meant for use on either straight or curved edges, as the illustrations show. A vernier adjustment is provided for extremely fine settings, *Fig. 5*, and is most useful

on the occasions when it is necessary to take another pass at the work to widen a groove or housing a fraction. A removable straightedge provided with the guide, has a cut-out in the centre to allow the bit to pass when making edging cuts. When cutting grooves or housings this straight section is left in place and runs along the edge of the work, an end cutting bit being used. If it is required to mould the edge of curved work this straight piece is taken off as the router will run easily along a curve.

Fig. 3   Front of Stanley router showing depth setting arrangements. Air intake holes above

Fig. 4   Depth of cut indicator, Stanley 267

**Fig. 5   Black and Decker router fitted
with straight and circular guide. Note
vernier adjuster on further rod**

It will at times be necessary to
make grooves or housings which are
too far from the edge of the work to
permit the use of the guide, and in
these circumstances there are two
other methods which can be employed. A bridge type jig can be made
up, as in *Fig. 6*, this being clamped
to the work and the router run
through it; or a batten half an inch
or so thick can be clamped across the
work and the router run along its
edge. If the latter method is used
it will be necessary to measure
the distance between the edge of the
router base and the edge of the
cutter, the batten being fixed accordingly. As with many other cutting
tools, the router can cause spelching
where it breaks out at the end of a
cross grain cut, and where there is
danger of this happening a piece of
scrap wood should be clamped on
to prevent it.

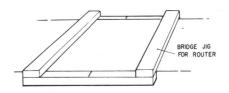

**Fig. 6   Bridge jig for router. Used
mainly in cutting housings**

The router will cut through or
stopped housing with equal ease,
Fig. 7, but in making a stopped
housing it is best to let the cutter enter
a short distance from the start of the
housing, bring it back to the starting
point, and then go through with the
cut to the other end. This ensures
accuracy, *Fig. 8*.

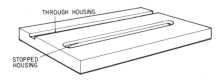

**Fig. 7   Through or stopped housings
are child's play with a router**

An increasingly popular use of routers
among amateurs is in the freehand
cutting of name boards for houses.
This is far from difficult, but does
require some practice before it can
be done quickly with a professional

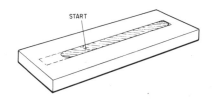

**Fig. 8   Method of making stopped
housings**

name is written on the board with a felt pen or similar instrument, and the cutting can be done. The normal procedure after cutting is to fill in the lettering with paint—black, red, gold, or whatever, and then sand the surface after the paint has dried, finishing off with varnish. In this sort of work particularly, the beginner will notice how the tool works differently according to the direction of the grain, but he will soon become accustomed to this.

finish. A vee grooving bit or a small cove bit will be used, the projection from the router base being about one-eighth of an inch. If you merely want to make one name board for your own house, there will be no rush about the job, but if you make a business of it you will soon find that the cutting becomes remarkably quick. It helps to make a tidy job if the work has been planed on one side and then passed through a thicknesser, *Fig. 9*.

Some artistic ability is obviously an advantage at this stage, but here again, practice makes perfect. The

Fig. 10 shows how a router is used on a circular edge, the straight portion of the guide having been removed. This is a simple operation, but as in all router work attention must be paid to the direction in which the machine is moved. The shaft revolves clockwise, so the router under most circumstances will be moved from left to right. This is against the rotation of the cutter and means that the tool will tend to hold itself in to the work rather than to push away from it. The novice will no doubt feel awkward with the router at first, and perhaps a little apprehensive, but once he begins to understand how it should be treated, its operation becomes far simpler.

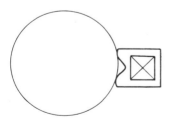

Fig. 10 When router is used on convex curves, the straight section of the guide is removed, so that the curved section has contact at two points

As with any other power tool, overloading the motor by taking cuts which are too heavy or by feeding too fast is bad. In the case of the router, however, the situation is further complicated by the fact that feeding too slowly is almost as bad.

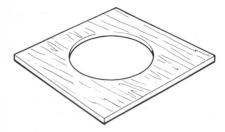

Fig. 11 Templates made from ply-wood or hardboard are widely used

Fig. 12 Dovetailing with the router. This is a form of template routing

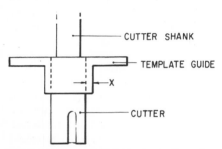

CUTTER SHANK

TEMPLATE GUIDE

X

CUTTER

Fig. 13 Template size must allow for the distance between cutter and outer face of guide, shown here at "X"

This is due to the very high speed of the tool; unless the cutter is fed at a fair rate it will burn the wood, over-heat itself, and may be spoiled permanently. Bits and cutters are not cheap, and this point has therefore to be watched. One soon learns to listen to the motor, and the correct rate of feed according to the depth of cut and material in use can be determined from this.

Template routing is also very popu-lar. By this means many identical shapes can be produced from a previously formed template of hard-board, plywood, or metal. The method may be used purely for decoration, for quick and accurate

outlining of an area which is to be routed out completely, as when sinking ceramic tiles and the like into wood, or for making items of a given shape by cutting right through the work. The purchaser of a router will be supplied with a handbook giving plenty of details. In fact, dove-tailing with a router is a very good example of template routing, *Fig. 12*, and some very attractive inlaid work can be done this way too. Before the router can be used in this manner, a template guide must be fitted to it, *Fig. 13*, and the template itself will have to be cut slightly over or under the required size to allow for the distance between the point where the outer edge of the guide touches the template, and the cutting edge of the bit. Whether the template is to be cut over or under size will obviously depend upon whether the cut is internal or external, and a little thought will soon sort this out.

It is possible to purchase planing attachments for routers, but these are normally only about 2 in. wide and

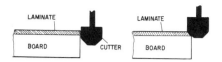

Fig. 14 Veneer trimming cutter giving square trim (left). Bevelled edge can be produced with the same cutter (right)

so their applications are limited.

Another useful accessory is the veneer trimming kit. With this fitted to the router, veneer, Formica, thin aluminium, or plywood, can be glued to a surface, leaving a slight overhang. The kit contains a cutter which has its edges tipped with tungsten carbide. This material is extremely hard and will last a long time but it is also brittle, so it should be treated with care. By virtue of its shape this cutter can be set to give a square flush trim, or a bevelled edge, Fig. 14, to the laminate, which is often desirable to prevent subsequent chipping. Complete instructions for use come with the kits, but the principle involved is that a

small wheel is set to run along the edge of the work and a fine screw thread adjuster is provided for absolute accuracy.

Basically there are two distinct types of cutters and bits for use with the router. The pilot type has a small extension below the cutter, see Fig. 16 (e, f, g). This runs along the edge and thus controls the cut. It is vital that the edge be prepared smooth since any inaccuracy will be reproduced by the pilot. In Fig. 16 (c) you can see a diagram of a two-fluted straight bit, which is both end and side cutting. This type of bit normally works with or across the grain, for cutting housings or grooves. It has no pilot, and the cut is controlled by means of a batten or the guide fence.

The photograph in Fig. 15 gives some idea of the range of jobs which the router will do, and the sketch,

Fig. 15 A selection of router cutters

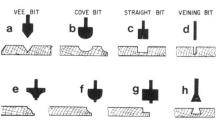

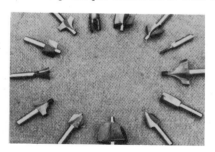

Fig. 16 Shapes of cutter showing their uses: a, vee bit—decorative cuts chamfer; b, cove bit—edge moulding, decorative cuts; c, straight bit—housings, routing out areas; d, veining bit—very narrow cut, mainly inlay work; e, pilot cutter—ovolo mouldings; f, pilot cutter—cove mouldings; g, pilot cutter—rebating; h, dovetail cutter

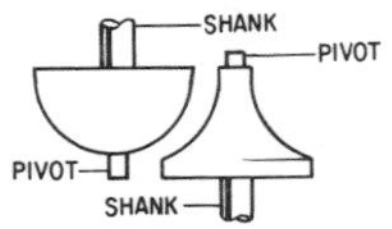

Fig. 17   Mating cutters for producing
drop leaf table joints

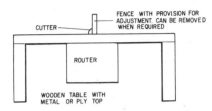

Fig. 18   Router can be mounted in
home made table

Fig. 16, illustrates some of the bits
and cutters and shows their purpose:
Incidentally, routers have become
almost an essential tool for joiners
and shopfitters, on account of their
ability to cut stair strings quickly and
accurately from a template, and for
veneer trimming on counters, cash
desks, and so on.

There is another type of tungsten
carbide tipped cutter which can be
used for veneer trimming. It gives a
bevelled edge, and its main advantage
is that it can work in areas where the
normal kit cannot be used, since it
has its own guide wheel. Drop leaf
table joints can be cut with a router
and special mating cutters can be
obtained for the job, *Fig. 17*.

The router can also be used as a
small spindle moulder with the aid of
a special table. As far as I am aware,
manufacturers of these tools do not
supply tables in which the router
can be inverted but such an item can
easily be made in the workshop, *Fig.
18*. There is one point to be considered when using a router in this
way, which is that small metal objects,
such as screws, nuts, and the like,
must be kept clear of the tool at all
times, since an object of this nature
could conceivably drop through the
ventilation apertures and considerable damage could result. This may

be one reason why the manufacturers
do not encourage the process but if a
little care is exercised there is no
problem.

A router set up in this way will
be found more useful for a number of
jobs where it is easier to move the
work than the tool. The table can be
made to individual taste but it should
be strongly constructed, and preferably mounted on a board so that it
can be clamped firmly to the bench
when in use. A wooden fence is
fitted, and constructed in such a way
that it can be moved to any required
position and locked by means of
bolts and wing nuts. Routing operations can thus be carried out on the
extreme edges of the work or at any
distance in from the edge.

Some forms of template routing,
especially where the work is relatively
small, can be carried out better with
the router mounted like this, the
template being under the work, and
riding against the template guide in
the usual way. An example of this
might be the routing out of wooden
squares to take decorative ceramic
tiles, using a two-fluted straight

cutting bit and holding the work firmly down to the table.

Another attachment which considerably widens the scope of the tool is the trammel point, which will enable accurate circle cutting to be undertaken. This is in two parts, a flat plate which is bolted in position across the base of the router, and the trammel point itself. The latter is an angled piece of metal with a sharp steel point. To fit this, the actual straight and circular guide is removed from the two rods together with the screw of the vernier adjuster, which can be unscrewed quite easily after the spring clip has been taken off. These parts should be put in a safe place, or they will almost certainly disappear into the sawdust and general rubbish. The bar which normally carries the vernier adjuster is used to mount the trammel attachment by means of a screw which is provided, and it should be noted that this can be fitted either with the point inwards towards the cutter for circles of small diameter, or facing outwards away from the cutter, when making large circles. The plate across the router base simply compensates for the thickness of the trammel section, so that the tool will be level on the work.

Perfect circles can be cut with this attachment, either partly into the wood for decorative or inlaid work, or right through. The depth of cut should be studied so that the router is not overloaded nor the cutter overheated, but the practical uses of this arrangement are important. Apart from a lathe I do not know of any power tool which will produce perfect circles, all of equal size if required, and this can be a big asset to the toy maker. I recently cut a large number of wheels for toys from $\frac{3}{8}$ in. ply, using a $\frac{1}{4}$ in. tungsten tipped cutter in conjunction with the trammel attachment, taking cuts of approximately $\frac{1}{8}$ in. depth at a time, and the wheels required nothing more than a rub with abrasive paper before they were used.

As an exercise in the use of the router with its trammel guide, and in the routing out of a background as is often done by wood carvers, why not try a simple coffee table top? You could use plywood, but solid wood would be better. This is illustrated in *Fig. 19.*

Starting off with a 24 in. square of wood we find the centre by drawing in the diagonals, then place the trammel point in the wood at the intersection and adjust the guide to give us a circle which will leave a minimum of $1\frac{1}{2}$ in. gap to the outside edge. With a vee grooving bit in the router set to cut lightly, say about $\frac{3}{32}$ in. deep, this circle is marked out. The cut is light so the router can be moved round quite quickly.

It is as well to make sure before beginning any trammel work with the router that there is nothing likely to foul the router or the rods, such as clamps or vices. When this has been done the router is laid aside for a few minutes while we draw two lines through the centre of the circle, at right angles to each other, thus dividing the circle into quarters. This is a simple geometric pattern, and no

Fig. 19 Simple design for table top which can be made with router and trammel attachment

or something similar is placed underneath to save damage to cutter or bench. A $\frac{1}{4}$ in. straight bit is used, taking cuts of $\frac{1}{8}$ in. at a time, and increasing the depth by this amount until the bit breaks through. The hatched areas shown in the pattern will be routed out by hand using a small straight bit and working to a depth of about $\frac{3}{32}$ in., leaving the extreme corners to be dealt with by means of a chisel afterwards. There are endless variations to this and it is given merely as an example, but it is one way of making the router pay for itself. The keen man will make himself a set of Queen Anne legs, but since these can be bought quite cheaply it is hardly worth the effort.

doubt other and better ones will occur to the user as he becomes used to the tool. Leaving the radius setting on the trammel as it is, the point is pushed into the wood at the end of one of the lines and an arc swung from edge to edge, which will, of course, pass through the centre. If care is taken in the setting of the trammel point each time, it is now only necessary to move round the circle, taking the arcs from the ends of the previous cuts.

This will result in a twelve "leaf" motif as in *Fig. 19*, with twelve smaller "leaves" in the middle. Changing over to a cove cutting bit the radius is extended, with the trammel point in the centre of the circle, to cut a groove midway between the edge of the design and the point at which the final circle will be cut out. This final cutting out obviously goes right through the wood, so a piece of scrap blockboard

Before leaving the subject of routers we should perhaps pay a little attention to the subject of cutting dovetail joints, an operation at which this tool really excels by virtue of its extremely high speed. Here again, for the man who makes furniture to sell, is a means of justifying the purchase of what is undoubtedly an expensive piece of machinery.

Dovetailing kits are available from the manufacturers and although they look very complicated they are in fact simple to use, and both fast and effective. This is, as will be seen, a form of template routing, the finger template supplied being made from a material which resembles *Tufnol*. It must be borne in mind that the cutter used is wider at the tip than the grooves or slots in the template, therefore the router must be slid into and out of the work, never lowered in or lifted out, unless you want to ruin a template. Full instructions for the use of these dovetail kits are supplied, but I will explain the process for the benefit of anyone who may be considering buying one.

Normally two sizes of template and cutter are available for the cutting of large or small dovetails, and it is important to see that the correct template guide is fitted to the router for the template in use. The basic part of the jig should be screwed to a board so that it can be clamped to the bench when required for use, and should project slightly forward of the bench edge. At each end of both the vertical and horizontal faces there are small pins which are vital to the job, and these can be moved into alternative holes according to the size of cutter and template being used. Care must therefore be taken to see that they are correctly positioned, which is not difficult since the threaded holes are numbered to correspond with the number on the template guide.

One of the critical settings is obviously that of the projection of the cutter from the router base, which will determine whether the joint is tight or loose. The usual thing is to set up by a trial and error method in the first instance, and then set the gauge supplied with the kit so that a quick setting can be made in future.

Another setting which is critical is that of the template itself, which can be brought toward or away from the operator by turning two nuts. The ideal setting will leave the dovetail pins just slightly proud so that they can be trimmed with a block plane, or sanded, after the joint is assembled.

The template guide is fitted to the router together with the appropriate cutter, and a few trial joints made before going ahead with the project, so that any necessary adjustments can be made.

It should be noted that the joints are cut inside out, so the box or drawer is first marked on its inside faces. The face edges also being marked. As long as you remember that the face edges must go against the pins and that the marks on the wood must be outward, you will not be able to make mistakes.

The template guide must be kept in contact with the template throughout the cut, and it is as well to go back over the cutting to make sure it is trimmed clean. The piece of wood which is clamped vertically is first put roughly in place so that the second piece, which is clamped horizontally, can be accurately positioned flush to it. When this has been done, the first piece is repositioned so that it is exactly level with the upper face of the second, and a check is made to ensure that both pieces are in contact with the pins. The clamps must be applied firmly so that there is no possibility of the work moving during the cutting. The template is put in place, pressing it down on the wood lightly while its clamp screws are tightened.

By virtue of the fact that the face edges of the pieces must contact the pins, two joints of a box or drawer are cut on the right hand side of the jig, and the remaining two on the left, but if the wood has been correctly marked in the first place this will be self evident.

CHAPTER 11

Dowelling with power tools

WE have seen how many woodworking joints can be cut quickly and easily with various power tools but I would like to deal with the question of dowelling separately, because it has assumed much more importance in recent years with the advent of synthetic resin adhesives—which are a far cry from the old style animal glue. A properly executed dowelled joint made with these adhesives has tremendous strength, is simplicity itself to make with the right tools, and takes very little time, once the job is set up. Old dowelling systems have gone now, there is no longer any need to mess around with pin heads and other bright ideas for aligning dowel holes, for there are a number of very good and reliable jigs on the market which take all the guesswork out of it and make the process easy.

Before going into the practical side of dowelling I would just like to point out that for the man who has no other facilities for the job, excellent mortising can be done with these jigs, as the illustrations show. The mortice is first marked out, the jig located over it, and a hole drilled to the required depth. By repeating this process until the other end of the mortice is reached the joint can be cut easily, and a sharp chisel will soon clean it up.

Some jigs include a depth gauge which can be clamped to the drill bit, but I still prefer the old dodge of wrapping a piece of adhesive tape round the drill. Provided the timber has been prepared square throughout, there should be no problem in using any of these jigs. There are six drilling guides with the *Stanley* jig, in sizes ranging from $\frac{3}{16}$ in. to $\frac{1}{2}$ in., and larger ones can be obtained should they be needed. The jig itself will fit timber up to $2\frac{7}{8}$ in. thickness, and the clamping plate has holes ready drilled in it so that a strip of wood can be attached to prevent marking the work. Each jig comes with complete instructions so I will not go into too much detail here.

The method of dowelling with a universal machine such as the *Coronet Major* may be of interest, since in principle it applies to other machines also. The illustrations covering this job are almost self-explanatory, but just in case the procedure is as follows. A Jacobs chuck is mounted in the mandrel of the machine, and in it is

Fig. 1 Stanley
dowelling jig shown
with guides, drills,
depth stops, and
dowels

Fig. 2 Dowelling jig
with turret head,
by Spiralux

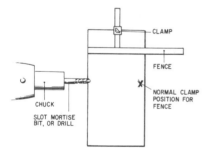

Fig. 3 Diagram showing dowelling
on Coronet Major. Note use of support
table, and that the fence has been
moved so that it is parallel with bit

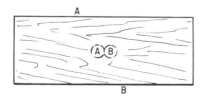

Fig. 4 Place wood on table and slide
up to revolving cutter, then turn it
over and repeat. Adjust table height
until marks will coincide

secured a drill bit of the appropriate
size. A suitable speed for drilling is
selected, and the support or combination table is brought into use.
Normally, as we saw earlier, this
table is used with its fence at right
angles to the bed of the lathe, but for
dowelling the fence is removed from
this position and replaced as shown
in *Fig. 3*. It is, of course, vital to
ensure that the drill bit is at ninety
degrees to the table, and that the
fence is parallel to the drill.

With this method of dowelling,
and indeed with others, the wood
should have first been passed through
a thicknesser so that no margin is left
for error. Assuming that 2 in. by 1 in.
material is being dowelled up into
frames, may be we require the dowel
holes to be 1 in. apart and in the
centre of the material. The latter
point is arrived at by trial and error
with regard to the height at which
the table is set, and a good tip in this
respect is shown in *Fig. 4*.

A piece of sticky tape is now
wrapped round the drill to give a
guide as to depth, and a piece of wood
exactly 1 in. wide and having parallel
sides, is placed against the table
fence. The wood being dowelled is
placed against this and slid into the
drill to the required depth. Now the

1 in. piece of wood is removed, and the work placed against the fence. The drilling is repeated, and we have two holes exactly 1 in. apart. This is easy enough on the end grain, but when the holes are drilled into the side of a rail there can be some difficulty in keeping the work square to the drill. This is best overcome by using a fairly wide board as a pusher,

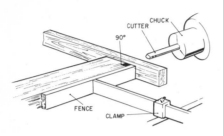

Fig. 5 Use a square ended board to feed rails to the drill when dowelling

Fig. 5, but be sure that the end of this board is truly square. Once this method has been practised a time or two it will come very easily and excellent results can be achieved.

There is hardly sufficient material in the subject of dowelling to make up an entire chapter, so I would like to continue with one or two other, totally unrelated, but nevertheless important things.

First among these is the jigsaw, which is a very good tool indeed if used properly, and various examples are shown in the illustrations. The blade of a jigsaw has a reciprocal action, and there is one advantage

over the bandsaw in that internal cuts can be made. The jigsaw is either allowed to peck its own way through the work, *Fig. 6*, or starting and turning holes can be drilled, or put in with a chisel mortiser if the corners are square. This is a really excellent tool for the toy maker, and if smooth edges are required they can be obtained by using a fine-toothed blade.

Fig. 6 Bosch jigsaw pecking its way through a plank, pivoted on toes of sole plate

A wide range of blades can be purchased for the cutting of wood, metal, and plastics, and it is important to use the right one for the job in hand. The cutting action of the tool is such that it cuts on the upstroke, so the blade tends to keep the sole plate in close contact with the work surface.

Some of the jigsaw attachments for electric drills are quite good, but it should be borne in mind that these are intended for occasional use. If you want a jigsaw to work for hours on end, then an industrial self-powered version should be purchased. Coarse blades cut fast, leaving a fairly rough edge which does not

Fig. 7 A good jigsaw will cut several
thicknesses at one pass

cutting of circles, but once the user has the feel of the tool he will cut better circles by freehand methods.

Jigsaws normally cut to a maximum thickness of two inches, and since there is no provision for lessening the projection of the blade when cutting thinner material this must obviously be clamped over the bench with blocks to raise it up, so that the sawblade will not strike any obstruction. Always see that the work is clamped securely, because some pressure has to be put behind the tool. If the material with which you are working is thin, it may be possible to cut out several pieces at the same time, clamping or nailing them together, *Fig. 7.*

matter if the work is to be sanded afterwards; fine blades cut slowly, but the finished edge is smooth.

This is a tool which is intended to be guided to a marked line. Like the bandsaw it tends to be inaccurate if used with guide fences and the like. Trammel points, or arms with points at the end, can be obtained for the

As with the portable router, a little ingenuity will enable the worker to devise and construct a sawtable for the jigsaw so that the blade comes up through the top surface and the work can be taken to the saw. For some work this is far more convenient than taking the tool to the job. The sole plate can be removed for this, and the screws which normally hold it in place used to fix it in the table.

Fig. 8 Stanley-
Bridges variable speed
jigsaw

Different makes of jigsaw have different features, and you will note that the *Stanley Bridges* saw illustrated has a variable speed control, which is useful where various types of material are to be cut. The *Bosch* saw, on the other hand, has an ingenious device for altering the rake of the blade. The coarser this is set, the faster the tool will cut, and vice versa.

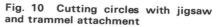

Fig. 10 Cutting circles with jigsaw and trammel attachment

Fig. 9 Bosch jigsaw with shaped rasps, and showing blade orbit adjusting lever

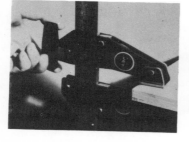

Fig. 12 Clamp heads reversed to push outwards

Fig. 11 The powerful and versatile "Jet" clamps

Fig. 13 Webbing clamps from CeKa tools

Accessories for this saw include a set of rasps, *Fig. 9*.

To conclude this chapter I would like to draw the attention of the reader to the *Jet* clamps, *Fig. 11*. You may have noticed these in use in various photographs earlier in the book, and I find them excellent. They are a *Gorle-White* product from *Eildon Marketing Services* of Coventry, and they are certainly superior to any other type of clamp I have used. The bar on which they slide is a standard size of bright steel, which of course gives them great versatility, since long lengths of this bar can easily be obtained. They come in pairs, and as you can see, one piece has a turnscrew on top of it. They can be moved to any required position on the bar by leaning them back against a spring and sliding them along. Final tightening is done by means of the turnscrew, and very heavy pressure can be applied. The clamps come supplied with three different types of snap-on jaw so the correct one can be selected for the material in use, and they have a further advantage in that they can be used internally to push outwards, *Fig. 12*. Whilst on the subject of cramps, the webbing belt type, such as the *Stanley* and the *CeKa, Fig. 13*, is also extremely useful.

CHAPTER 12

Care of the cutting edges

CERTAIN of our power tools will be kept sharp by the use of a file, such as circular saw-blades, while others will need to be taken to the grindstone. It would be a wonderful thing if we could all have at our disposal a wet stone, revolving slowly and with water running over it! For most of us this just cannot be, on the grounds of expense, space in the workshop, and so on, and so we must do what we can with small carborundum wheels. Let me say at once that there is nothing wrong with these wheels, but they cut fast and generate a lot of heat in the process, so they must be used with care if the temper of the tool is not to be destroyed. I use a Wolf double-ended grinder, *Fig. 1*, and I have nothing but praise for it; when using it I work slowly and keep a pot of water handy so that I can dip the tools in from time to time.

No attempt should ever be made to hurry the job of grinding tools, for they are expensive, and easily damaged by unskilled use of a grinder. Safety is a matter for consideration here too, and it is vital that the grinder is never used without adequate protection for the eyes. Professional woodworkers never grudge the time taken to sharpen cutting tools, whereas unfortunately the amateur frequently looks upon this as a waste of time, and continues to work with blunt edges. This can be dangerous, but even if no injury results to the operator, damage is quite likely to be done to the motor,

Fig. 1 Eight-inch double-ended grinder by Wolf

Fig. 2 Freshening up a glazed wheel with a "devil" stone

surface of the wheel to become glazed. When this happens the wheel no longer cuts freely and unnecessary heat is generated. A small "devil stone", *Fig. 2*, applied hard to the revolving grinding wheel will cut away the surface and put matters right.

Since this book deals essentially with power tools, I will not enter into a discussion on the grinding of hand tools such as chisels and screwdrivers, but we do have to sharpen twist drills, and this is a very difficult art which some men never really master. I would love to be able to explain in simple language exactly how it should be done but I fear it is one of those things which come with practice and experience. The process is shown in *Fig. 3*, and there are basically two main points on which the novice falls down. The first of these is that when new a twist drill will have two cutting edges of equal length. Examination of such a drill after inexperienced grinding is likely to reveal the fact that one edge has become longer than the other. Obviously this means that the point of the drill is no longer central, and the hole produced by it will be inaccurate. The second point is that twist drills are relieved behind their cutting edges so that it is the cutting edge which contacts the work, not the whole of the drill point. If we were dealing with metal working I would consider it advisable to go into far greater detail on this, but for use on wood the drills need not be so

Fig. 3 Sharpening a twist drill on the Wolf grinder

which is working far harder than it should. The grinding wheel itself needs some care and if it is to work satisfactorily nothing but tools or clean metal should be ground on it. The grinding of soft metals such as aluminium or brass, wood, plastic materials and the like will cause the exact. There are in fact better types of boring tools than the twist drill, as far as the woodworker is concerned, a number of these being shown in the illustrations.

With reference to the various cutters for planers, router cutters, and other high speed steel tools, the amateur will be well advised to make no attempt to grind these, but to return them to the manufacturer where they will be sharpened on special machines, the cost being very reasonable.

I earn my living by writing about and teaching the use of woodturning lathes and light woodworking machines. I have men coming to me for tuition from long distances, and I doubt very much whether, of the many I have taught, more than about one in ten was capable of tackling the sharpening of a circular sawblade. To me this seems a great pity, for there is really no magic attached to it at all. The man who has his own sawbench relies upon his blades to help him achieve the precision and accuracy he strives for, and this would bring him even greater satisfaction if he learned to look after his own blades. I am not by any means suggesting that every man should become a saw doctor for this is a highly skilled job, but part of the process of keeping blades in good condition is within the capabilities of any man of average intelligence.

I will try, therefore, by words and illustrations to explain the simpler parts of the job, and I will try not to get too deep into technicalities. The real crux of the matter is that there will come a time for almost every amateur when his blade needs to be sent away for a complete overhaul, but my point is that this need not happen anything like as often as it does. Blades for circular saws, whether drill-driven or self-powered, are made by saw manufacturers, specialists in fact, and not normally by the makers of the driving equipment, and a great deal of research has gone into this over the years. For this reason it is often advocated that when a new sawblade is acquired, its exact shape should be reproduced on paper by drawing round it with a fine pencil and every effort should be made to keep that shape.

If a circular saw blade has been allowed to get really bad, the first operation which should be carried out is the stoning of the blade. There is some controversy about this, as some say that the saw should be mounted as when in normal use, while others like myself prefer to have the sawblade running backwards. The table is set so that the teeth of the saw have only a minute projection above the insert, this being checked with a piece of scrap wood before beginning the stoning process. When all is ready, the motor is started, and a coarse oilstone moved slowly along the rip fence so that it cuts down the teeth. There is no danger here, but keep a firm grip on the stone. The blade should now be examined carefully, and bright marks will be found on top of most, or all, of the teeth. If any have escaped the stone the table is lowered by a mere whisker and the operation repeated. At this juncture some teeth

118

Fig. 4   Wooden discs clamped either side of the blade will support it while it is filed

will have been ground down more than others.

The blade can now be removed from the machine, as the remainder of the treatment is with a file, the blade being held between two discs of wood in a vice, *Fig. 4*. Some workers advocate the blackening of the teeth with a candle flame so that the file strokes can be studied better. This may assist those with poor eyesight, but I never bother myself. The idea of the circular wooden "sandwich", of which the blade forms the "meat", is to give support to the teeth whilst they are being filed.

Please don't use just any old file for this job. The gullets of the blade are very important and their shape must be retained, so a mill file is used and preferably one which fits the gullets. It will be found best to file the teeth which are leaning away from you, which means taking alternate teeth and then reversing the saw in the vice and repeating the procedure. On the type of blade in most common use in home workshops, which is the combination rip and crosscut, the file is used straight across the front of the teeth, at right angles to the blade.

For the benefit of anyone who has not been taught how to use a file correctly, the method is to press the tool against the metal and push it slowly forward. I have seen files used on many occasions much as a violinist

would use his bow in playing a jig, and this sort of thing must be avoided. After one or two slow strokes with the file the face of the tooth is examined, and if it has been cut all over, the next tooth can be done. If there are any dull spots, however, these indicate that the file has not touched and they must be removed. Sharpening a saw in this manner retains the depth of gullet, which was put there for a purpose, whereas if only the tops of the teeth are filed, the gullets will be reduced each time. When all the teeth have received this treatment we start all over again, this time filing the tops. Here, again, the teeth which lean away are dealt with first, the blade being reversed to complete the job. You will find that the tops of the teeth are ground at an angle of about ten degrees and it is important to keep this angle if you can. File slowly across the teeth, and make sure that each one is filed. In this process the idea is to file away all the flats which were produced by stoning, though you may find that some teeth no longer have a flat, this having been removed in filing the gullets. These can be left alone. The set of the teeth is best left to an expert.

CHAPTER 13

Some other machinery

NO book dealing with modern power tools would be complete without the two machines described in this chapter; namely the *De Walt* radial arm saw, and the *Burgess Emco Star* universal machine. I mentioned the *Emco Star* earlier in general terms, but it is too interesting a tool to be treated in a sketchy manner.

This machine is a very interesting and ingenious piece of equipment, but unfortunately, in common with many other power tools, it is difficult to find a tool shop where it is thoroughly understood and an explanation of its workings can be obtained. It does have one striking point in its favour, in that the instruction book supplied with it is very detailed indeed, which is as it should be—other manufacturers please note! It is nicely finished, capable of serious work, and worthy of a place in any home workshop.

Extra accessories can be purchased for the machine and I will describe these in due course, but the basic machine consists of a circular saw, a bandsaw, a belt sander, and a disc sander. All of this is built into one single unit, with a drive shaft and coupling for the *Emco Rex* planer, if this should be purchased. It should be noted that all the items mentioned above can be used without the necessity for dismantling the machine, or in fact using any spanners. Changing over from bandsaw to circular saw is simply a matter of pivoting the machine, an action which automatically disengages the drive to the saw which is out of use.

The bandsaw cuts very well, but the throat is restricted to some extent by the rise and fall knob for the circular saw, as the photographs show. It is still a very useful tool, nonetheless. The circular saw has a depth of cut of just over 2 in., which suffices for most home users, and it performs very well indeed. The blade supplied is an *Amersaw* made by the American Saw Co., and it holds its edge for a considerable time. The sawtable can be tilted to forty-five degrees and is equipped with a guard and a rip fence. There is also a slot in the table for a mitre gauge.

The disc sander has a clockwise rotation. As with all disc sanders of this type the work is applied to the downward moving part of the abrasive so that it tends to be held

Fig. 1   Fitting
eccentric cam drive to
Emco Star for jig and
fretsaw

to the table, and the rubbish is not flung up at the operator. Its companion, the small belt sander, is a useful little device.

The two available speeds, according to the instruction book, are 3,000 rpm at ¾hp, and 1,500 rpm at ½hp. The slower of these should be used when sanding or too much heat will be generated, causing burning of the work. When using the belt sander, the rip fence on the saw table can be moved across and used as a guide.

Two other items which I would recommend to those who have a use for them as being useful and reliable are the jigsaw and the fretsaw. These are attachments, inasmuch as a certain amount of time must be spent in preparation before they can be used. *Fig. 1* shows that these tools are driven by an eccentric cam mounted on the arbor of the circular saw, and a little light machine oil should be applied occasionally. I must admit that when I first looked at an *Emco Star* I was not too impressed by these two saws, but

when I actually put them to use I changed my opinion rapidly, *Fig. 2.* For the man who makes models or toys, they are ideal and run very smoothly, see *Ch. 3, Fig. 11.* They will handle hard or soft woods very well indeed, and I find the fretsaw particularly useful. There are some other accessories available which will convert the machine for drilling, spindle moulding, grinding, polishing, and mortising; should you require it a flexible shaft can be obtained.

The radial arm saw is another matter altogether. It is the sort of machine which practically any home woodworker would love to own, and if he could get the opportunity to try one out fully I do not think he would rest until he owned one. Unfortunately it is not an easy tool to describe successfully to anyone who is not familiar with its principles, and you will see that I have had to use rather more illustrations than for most other machines. Looking at one of these

Fig. 2 Power driven fretsaws such
as the Bosch Combi shown here, and
the Emco Star, can save hours of work

in a shop window is really rather a
waste of time, unless you have someone with you who can explain things,
and if you go into the shop to look at
it, this may make matters even worse!
Fortunately there is a very compre-
hensive stiff covered book which can
be bought dealing with the use
of the saw in tremendous detail, so
things are not too bad. As you look
at it, the machine appears to be
smothered with adjusting knobs,
levers, thumbscrews, and whatever,
not to mention graduated scales, but
if you read the instruction book you
will soon see that it is by no means as
complicated as it looks.

The machine I have used for purposes of illustration has a 10 in.
diameter sawblade, giving a 3 in.
depth of cut. There is no lack of
power in the motor, and anyway this
is given the normal protection of a
thermal overload cut-out. Not without some trepidation, I will now
attempt to describe the construction
of the tool, and how it works. This
is far from easy, but if the text is
taken with the photographs there
should be no real difficulty.

The base of the machine is strongly
constructed of metal with a thick
plywood table mounted on it. Many
users cover this with a thin sheet of
ply so that it does not become covered
in saw marks, but this is a matter of
choice. You can see that at the rear
of the table a stout metal column
rises vertically, and upon this is
mounted the radial arm carrying the

saw and motor, these being mounted
on a yoke assembly which carries
them backwards or forwards along
the arm as required. If I now tell you
that the yoke can be pivoted through
360 degrees, and that the motor can
be swung between the arms of the
yoke, you will begin to see what I
meant about difficulty of description.

The arm carrying the motor and
saw assembly can be swung in an arc
over the table and locked in any
desired position by means of a lever.
The forty-five degree positions are
automatically located, and these are
exact, which makes the cutting of
mitres a very simple job. The angle
at which the saw has been set is
shown in the little window on the end
of the arm, and any angle can be set
with complete accuracy. In *Fig. 3*,
the end of a board is being trimmed
off at an angle, and if a compound
angle cut is required the motor
would be tilted in its position inside

Fig. 3   Trimming off end of board at an angle

the yoke. There are clamp handles on the machine to lock it at any setting, and these must be retightened before cutting. In *Fig. 4* a board is being ripped. The ninety degree positions have positive location.

The other very important movement with the radial arm saw is of course the raising and lowering of the arm in order to adjust for depth of cut, and this is shown in *Fig. 5*. There is a handle on top of the arm, in this case towards the front, (although with some machines it is at the rear), and one complete turn of this handle will raise or lower the arm exactly one-eighth of an inch. It will be readily appreciated that this is a precision control, since a quarter of a turn gives a movement of one thirty second of an inch. This control is very useful indeed when working

on top of the wood, as in making housing for shelves, *Fig. 6*. Another factor is that since the sawblade is mounted directly on the motor shaft there is never any question of power loss through belt slip, and 3 in. hard-woods can be cut with ease.

The wooden table top is made in three sections. There is a wide piece at the front with the fence behind it, and there are two more pieces to the rear of the fence. At the front of the table there are two adjustable clamps which hold this whole assembly rigid. These can be released when necessary and the fence then positioned further back, an operation which will be necessary when ripping wide stock. When the machine is new it is equipped with a fence, but this is most definitely an expendable item, and if like myself you do a lot of angle cutting and dado work it will eventually become so badly cut about that it must be replaced. This is a simple matter, as a length of 2 in. by 1 in. softwood will do, though taller fences have their uses in some operations.

Throughout this book I have tried to stress safety points, and in connection with this particular tool there is one point which cannot be too strongly stressed, this being that the

Fig. 4   Ripping with the radial arm. Wood is fed to the saw

Fig. 5   The radial arm
can be raised and
lowered by means of
the special handle

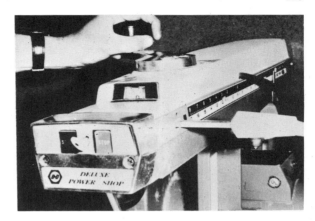

saw must be returned to the back of the fence after every cut. It is extremely dangerous to neglect this and I believe there is a device which can be purchased to pull the saw back automatically. It will be obvious when you think about it that if the revolving blade is left overhanging the table slightly the next piece of wood can be grabbed by it, and a bad injury to the hands could result. The model shown has a built-in brake to stop the blade in a few seconds when the motor is switched off, but on some other machines there may be a manually operated button for this.

The actual use of the saw bears little resemblance to the use of an ordinary sawbench. The photographs cover it fairly well, and you will see that in ripping and grooving cuts, the saw is held stationary on the arm and the material fed beneath it. On the other hand, cross cutting, bevel crosscutting, and trenching require the material to be kept still against the fence and the saw pulled along the arm, *Fig. 7.*

Fig. 6   Through
housing being cut with
dado head

Fig. 7 **Material is held stationary against fence when crosscutting. Saw is pulled through**

Fig. 8 **"In-rip" position. Saw remains stationary and work is fed from spring heel end**

Fig. 9 **De Walt saw in "out-rip" position on wide board. Two different models of this saw are seen in this chapter's illustrations**

Never under any circumstances use a radial arm saw without its guard. This is the heighth of folly, and anyone injured in such a manner has no-one to blame but himself.

When making cuts which pass right through the wood the sawblade is set so that the teeth are approximately $\frac{1}{16}$ in. below the surface of the wooden table. The newcomer to radial saws will find that crosscutting requires a little practice. The bottom of the sawblade is revolving towards the fence, and so the saw is inclined to "walk" through the wood. This tendency has to be resisted, but it soon becomes second nature. This type of saw is in its element with any form of compound angle cutting, which is simply a matter of making the necessary settings and pulling the saw through.

Ripping with the radial arm saw is not quite as straightforward as one might think, in fact I personally prefer a normal bench for this sort of work, but I will describe the method as it is interesting. There are two distinct set-ups for ripping, as shown in *Figs. 8* and *9*. The "in-rip" position is the one most used, but the "out-rip" setting will be necessary when cutting down a wide piece of material. Saws of this nature are not really at their best in ripping work, principally because the teeth of the blade are coming upwards through the wood, but when the technique has been mastered they will do good work. Along the side of the arm are two scales, one for setting the machine when in-ripping and the other for out-ripping.

In setting up the tool for either of these operations, the procedure must be followed faithfully or there may well be trouble. A study of the illustrations will help to clarify what follows. On the heel of the saw guard is a small spring, and an adjustable rod carrying a number of anti kick-back fingers. Note that the material must NEVER be fed to the saw from this end. When in-ripping the feed will be from right to left, and when out-ripping it will be from left to right. With the motor switched off, the material to be cut is placed under the heel of the guard, the saw having been positioned as required for the cut, and the guard is swung down so that the spring presses on the wood. The anti kick-back fingers are now adjusted so that they are about $\frac{1}{8}$ in. lower than the surface of the wood, and locked there. The cutting is easy enough, feeding the wood steadily to the blade along the fence from the opposite end to the spring, and completing the cut with a push stick.

One of the most useful accessories for the radial arm saw is without any doubt the dado head, *Fig. 10.* It is not cheap but it is well worth having. It

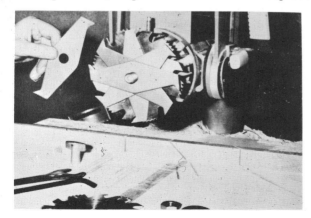

Fig. 10 A typical dado head being assembled

Fig. 11   Dado head in
use for decorative
cutting

Fig. 12   Recently introduced, the Coronet Consort. A good sawbench, to
which a wide variety of attachments
can be fitted

consists of two special sawblades, each ⅛ in. thick, and having no set to the teeth. There is also a set of chippers which can be seen quite clearly in *Fig. 10*, these being of varying thicknesses, and it is possible to make cuts varying from ⅛ in. up to $\frac{13}{16}$ in., increasing in stages of one-sixteenth. The dado head should be assembled as shown—do not have all the chippers lined up, they should be staggered. This is a very good accessory indeed for grooving, trenching, joint cutting, and the making of decorative cuts, *Fig. 11*.

As I have said, a complete book is available on the subject of this type of saw so I cannot possibly do justice to it here, but I hope I have suceeded in arousing some interest in it.

Index